D1171496

HOMEMADE PIZZA

Davide Civitiello

italiasquisita

Homemade Neapolitan pizza: how everything has begun

by ItaliaSquisita

It all started from a very tasty casatiello.
It was 2015 when ItaliaSquisita filmed Davide Civitiello for the first time. The enthusiasm, professionalism and educational talent of the young pizza maker immediately left their mark, giving life to a video that over the years has become a classic of Neapolitan cuisine on the web.

From that moment on, many doughs have risen, and there were many preparations that Davide wanted to recount in front of our cameras: holiday desserts, variations of classic and contemporary pizzas, calzoni, deep-fried pizzas and many of insights into the ingredients and techniques behind the most famous pizza in the world. A succession of memories, gestures and quantities that over time have built a real recipe book, technical and personal, which not only tells the past but also the future of Neapolitan pizza, through the style of one of its great interpreters.

However, the milestone of this journey was a specific video, shot in Posillipo in 2017, with the emblematic title 'Neapolitan homemade pizza'. A simple video tutorial, yet impossible for some, certainly unpublished until then, and which today we could define as 'historical' somehow. For the first time, a great professional from Campania developed a recipe and dedicated a video to homemade Neapolitan pizza. Was it a sacrilege? Even if the answer seems obvious to us, it certainly was a breaking video for the culture of the territory, and a risky and ambitious decision by Davide, to put his hand onto such an untouchable tradition. The video could have diminished and perhaps impoverished the aura of 'mystery and holiness' behind the world of Neapolitan pizza, but the results proved us right: it was a video thought for everyone, bursting with almost twenty years of experience, capable of putting an exclamation point on gastronomic edutainment in Italy and abroad. After all, it is the most globally viewed video about pizza released in the Italian language.

But that is not all. In addition to the huge public response, in a short time 'homemade Neapolitan pizza' has also became a trend in the contemporary pizza scene in Campania, and this was perhaps the greatest satisfaction for a professional like Civitiello.

This epic video, and all the material we fermented and rose together with Davide, now also finds an 'analogical expression': in fact, the work of these years comes in a wider and more complex space, where the professional's experience is trasmitted in an analytical way, beyond the limits of the video medium. A book, the one you are holding, which is therefore the culmination of a path modeled on the needs of the public but with the ambition to lead enthusiasts to a new level of practice and awareness of the pizza product. A book where Davide Civitiello has collected and explained through precious masterclasses all the styles and methodologies to make an authentic Neapolitan pizza in the domestic oven, with tips and tricks that come directly from his infinite professional adventures in Naples and around the world. A colorful journey into traditional doughs and toppings, seen through the gastronomic imagination of a great professional; a path that – thanks to the important contribution of his chef friend Antonio Sorrentino and various experts in the industry – was then extended to serveral risings technique, technical insights on ingredients, typical breads, desserts and holiday specialties, to show how pizza is the fundamental hub of a much larger and more ancient history, that of the baking art of Campania.

Finally, this is also the book by means of Davide Civitiello, for the first time, shows himself to the public not only as a professional and a character, but also through his own story, made of sacrifices, surprising encounters and an inexhaustible passion for new challenges.

Making love with the dough

by Davide Civitiello

This book contains everything: my life, my growth, my dreams and my hopes, my ideas, my failures, my gastronomic experiences and the road I had to cover to acquire all the knowledge I currently own. Here is all my travels around the world, all the people who have always believed in me, my partners. There is my family and, most of all, my pizzas. This book is who I am.

My name is Davide Civitiello, born 1984, and I have been living on pizza since I was 9 years old.

I started, as it often happens, partially for fun and partially out of need. My mother Anna used to work as a domestic assistant for the Costa family, owner of the historical pizzeria Da Gennaro located in 1, via Maddalena and, when I was out of school, especially over the summer holidays, I used to spend my free time between those walls that represented for me the most amusing playground: fires, flames, flours, doughs, basil, tomatoes, mozzarellas... Yes, I was born with the flavors, the sounds and the colors of pizza and pizzerias.

I was feeling crazy happy when I was there. While waiting for my mum to end her shift at their home, Vincenzo, the owner, provided me with a t-shirt with the logo of the pizzeria printed on it and used to make me run around the restaurant. I was forced to get the t-shirt into my trousers because, despite being the smallest size available, it fit unreasonably large on me. I used to wander around the pizzeria armed with a *chiavetta*, a very small bottle opener I used to uncork the drinks of the customers.

I became the mascot of the pizzeria, beloved and cuddled by everyone. Once I finished the third year of comprehensive school, I told my mother that I would interrupt my studies to dedicate all of myself to pizza. "When I grow up, I want to become a pizzaiolo!" And so, we made a deal: if I had been able to live on pizza from that moment up to the next 5 years, I could have continued following my dream for my entire life. And so it was.

This is my story and I want to tell it in the exact way I lived it, that is to say with all my body and soul.

The Neapolitan beginnings

The 'ground floor' is very hard in the world of catering, but at the same time there is nothing as fulfilling as receiving such satisfaction after so much effort. I began as a waiter, and then went on to carry out various tasks and jobs, from dishwasher to baker, through being the person in charge of the *staglio* phase – meaning the portioning of the balls of pizza dough. My job was to make sure nothing was missing for, the pizza makers, the ones I kept on looking up to with extreme

Davide at the pizzeria Da Gennaro
by Vincenzo Costa

respect and veneration. I was lucky enough to grow with solid principles and excellent models, such as my two elder siblings Michele, the oldest, and Francesco, the second-born who, since forever, have always pointed me towards the right way to live in this world: with humbleness and commitment.

At the time, pizzeria Costa was a pizzeria unlike the others, and represented a true pizza

Davide's master, and owner of the pizzeria Da Gennaro

factory: we used to produce between 1000 and 1500 pizzas a day! An enormity.

We were number one among the makers of pizza a *portafoglio*, a kind of pizza you eat as you walk, folded in 4 parts. Another specialty of ours was deep-fried pizza, pizza fritta, that, at the time, used to be served in paper packets – the famous *navetta* closed with a paper usually employed for wrapping up bread.

Yes, during the 'groundwork' I also spent some time making deep-fried pizzas, and I will never deny it – the compulsive repetition of those gestures have affected and influenced my stamina behind the counter.

Mister Vincenzo Costa, or more precisely, maestro Enzo, used to very often repeat that this job runs in my veins. I owe him a lot, from both a professional and – most of all – personal point of view.

He has always been my putative father and when he died, all my certainties began to vacillate more than ever. The absence of a direct debate with him almost pushed me to give everything up and go back to school. In that period I was a *battente* – that is to say the one in charge of stretching out the pizza for the pizzaiolo – and although on one side my professional growth was living a huge progression, on the other I felt the need of looking for new stimuli. At that point I knew every corner of that pizzeria and I should have waited for the retirement of the old pizzaiolos before having the chance to become head pizza maker and, most of all, I couldn't have done it under the watch of my master anymore. So, on the saddle of my motor-scooter, I decided to go away and to take some time to think over my future before making the next step.

The first encounter with Rossopomodoro

After a little while, my brother Michele phoned me and told me that a friend of his was looking for a pizza maker for the opening of a pizzeria in Piazza Dante, in the very heart of Naples. I came back from my holidays right away and the next day I showed up and introduced myself. The pizzeria had a very catchy name: Rossopomodoro. When I entered the room, I met a pizza maker named Antonio Bastelli. When I told him that I was 18, he could hardly believe it – "It is impossible to be 18 and... a pizzaiolo!" He thought I was far too young for the job, therefore he said goodbye and walked away. A few weeks passed and I had not received a call or any other kind of communication. So, I decided to go to the pizzeria and have a pizza.

When I sat down, my eye immediately fell behind the counter: there was a pizzaiolo, older than me, and he moved with dexterity and awareness. With my usual brazen face and with the arrogance of an 18 years old, I went straight up to Antonio, who recognized me immediately.

He told me that the pizzaiolo was a boy he had raised many years ago and he was now desperately looking for a baker. All of a sudden, he asked me: "Would you like to come and work as a baker on Saturday?" I accepted with no hesitation.

Saturday has always been the day of the most intensive work for a pizzeria in the historical center of Naples. We had a hundred orders both at the tables and for takeaway pizzas. Just the time to bake a Margherita and a Marinara, and Antonio enthusiastically told me that I would have worked there for a long time. From that moment on a new adventure began with Rossopomodoro. A reality that would have broadened my range of action exponentially, allowing my career to take a huge step towards my destiny: education and a technical-scientific approach to the world of pizza.

From Capri to Argentina

I had some very happy moments in that place. I perfected the techniques, the doughs, the recipes. I became a professional, so diligent and knowledgeable. But in spite of that, at that age, I felt that my will to grow had still not been satisfied enough and so, in my free time, I used to go around pizzerias and restaurants, looking for a little extra work. I was not driven by money, but something more precious: a hunger to learn. One day I found myself at the Trattoria/Pizzeria La Taverna del Re, run by Gianni Lotti, a fine sommelier and restaurateur. He gave me an opportunity to work at his place whenever I wanted and told me something truly important: "The way you

Davide during his first experience at Rossopomodoro in Piazza Dante

truly understand that you are able to do something is when you can actually do it on your own." I have been carrying those words inside me until today and, I believe, I will keep them with me for the rest of my life.

After 8 months of hustle, baking pizzas at Rossopomodoro and making dough at La Taverna del Re, one night, at the pizzeria in Piazza Dante a guy from Sri Lanka came in: his name was Fernando. It was almost midnight and outside it was pouring with rain. We worked very little that evening and we were just about to put the fire out in the oven. Fernando came in, soaked wet, and asked me to make him a saltimbocca. In spite of everything,

Davide with Donato De Santis and Pedro Picciau in Capri

I decided to feed him. Whilst I was cooking, he was staring at me with a massive smile on his face and told me very happily: "If my master sees you, he will give you loads of money". I pretended not to listen. However, while waiting for the *saltimbocca* to cook, Fernando said again: "If my master sees the way you work, he will give you loads of money". So, a question arose spontaneously: "My friend, who is your master?"

Well, that *saltimbocca* would have satisfied my hunger for knowledge.

Fernando's employer was mister Brunetti, owner of the restaurant Resto Wine Bar Pizzeria Agorà, on the beautiful island of Capri. That place, at the time, represented an out-and-out revolution in the gastronomic panorama of the island. A multi-ethnic restaurant that moved in a completely opposite way compared to the needs and offer of the island, so used to

sea-food dishes, typical products and wine. Chef Lello Sorrentino used to compose dishes using Thai and Indonesian rice, top quality Argentinian meat and high intensity cooking with the wok, that at the time was barely used not only in Capri, but throughout Italy. At the Brunetti family's restaurant you were able to eat dishes of all kinds: from spaghetti with tomato sauce to Cantonese rice. Mister Brunetti also wanted to offer a wide selection of pizzas and for this reason he was looking for a Neapolitan pizzaiolo.

So I decided to spend the summer season in Capri, and those have been among the most amazing and fun days of my life. Working with chef Sorrentino was stimulating in so many ways. His cuisine was experimental and he always used to bring new preparations in a menu that was constantly evolving to the point that it was challenging – of course – but also a drive to improvement, as well as to learn even more. At the very beginning, the demand for pizzas was quite scarce, so I dedicated myself to kitchen preparations: cutting and cooking vegetables, cutting the meat and, from that moment on, I started to conceive the idea of bringing the world of pizza and gastronomy together, thus setting off the beginning of my journey as an 'expert' on the matter.

Indeed, I became aware of that same feeling I had during my first experience at Rossopomodoro: I wanted to adopt a more technical and scientific approach towards the world of pizza. It was summer, I was young and, most of all, I was located on one of the most famous island in the world. One day, during a very pleasant night, I met two of Lello's dearest friends: Donato De Santis and Pedro Picciau, two great professionals in the world of cuisine, famous across all South America. They saw me cooking and making pizzas and, towards the end of the evening, they offered me a chance to join them in Argentina and to bring my pizza along with me. I believe that what convinced them was a phrase that came out of my mouth when Donato asked me: "How do you realize that the pizza dough is ready?" and I told him, unsettling him, "You have to make love to the dough".

With my pizzas and this sentence, I won over the heart and spirit of Donato De Santis, the most famous Italian chef in South America and personal chef of Gianni Versace for more than 20 years.

The summer of Capri was a dream, whilst the insular winter was harder to overcome unless you were used to it. That summer I made pizzas for entrepreneurs, journalists, and people from the show-biz. I even had the chance to make Keanu Reeves a pizza. But leaving Italy for the first time and experiencing such an opportunity was too good a chance to let it go to be missed and, at 22 years old, to go and work in the land of my undisputed idle – Diego Armando Maradona – was priceless. Thus my travelling time in life began. From that moment on, I never stopped.

Even today Lello Sorrentino is still one of my best friends and we are constantly in touch. I go back to Capri every time I can: by now, that island will always stay in my heart.

The first Neapolitan pizza-shows and the discovery of the refractory stone

I decided to travel to Argentina and spend a well-deserved holiday. I traveled around all of South America, and then I took a long break in Buenos Aires where Donato greeted me as if I was one of his children. We ate and drank together at his place in a wonderful garden.

We used to speak about cuisine and pizzas and we would journey across the most precious memories of our Capri days together. Donato then told me that he would shortly start shooting a tv show for a national broadcast.

I remember us sitting at the table, sipping a great root liqueur he had made. Donato looked straight into my eyes and said: "Would you like to come and be part of the show? I will be involved in a pizza show". And so I came back to Italy, with the hope of travelling back to Argentina.

After two months only, Donato kept his promise and invited me to his place again so as to join the tv program. I would have been

Davide with Lello Sorrentino in Capri
Davide in the kitchen in Capri with Lello, Donato and Mariano

a guest of honor in the episode related to Neapolitan pizza. Now, even though Argentina was a very hospitable land, at that time its cuisine did not include top quality grains. There was in fact a great abundance of flours with 4 or 5 zeros that almost resembled icing-sugar.

Some of these flours even came enriched with a dose of yeast. Therefore, I was obliged to reinforce flours with powdered gluten so as to guarantee a slow rising process and a pizza that could live up to the expectations.

I noticed that in Buenos Aires the refractory stone was often used for cooking any sort of dish. It was 2010 and, at the time, cooking a pizza with that specific method was almost sacrilegious. However, heedless of danger,

Davide during the recording of Pizza alla Donato, Buenos Aires (Argentina, 2013)

I decided to run a few experiments. I started considering various types of stone, studied them and chose a fairly thin one, not too thick.

The first attempts were disastrous but after a while, and a little practice, I began mastering this technique that, in time, has become one of my masterpieces. The refractory stone – as you will have the chance to learn in the following pages – lends the homemade pizza almost the same cooking consistency of a pizza oven.

Since then, I have been using this technique everywhere, also bringing it in a video-recipe that would have marked a crucial passage in my life as a gastronomic communicator. But this is a matter we will get to further ahead.

The day of the shooting, as soon as the crew got to Donato's, it began to rain. I thought to myself, "How lucky", all this traveling just

to give up the chance of being part of this show. Donato looked at me and, with his usual reassuring smile, he told me: "Don't you worry Davide – and just as any Italian would say – wet episode, lucky episode". And this time again, he was right. The shooting went on no matter the rain, in Donato's garden where the chef had built a wonderful wooden oven made with bricks. Completely by chance, that episode was broadcasted several times. For the occasion I had made 4 types of Margheritas, a roll filled with rocket, grana cheese, prosciutto and tomatoes; a panuozzo from Gragnano and a pizza with a stuffed cornicione. At the end of the shooting the troupe devoured everything – not a crumb was left. I spoke about the slow rising process, about the dough worked by hand and about the wooden cooking method.

It was the first time in front of a camera and after a brief moment of embarrassment, I must say, I felt completely at ease. Even though I didn't speak a word of Spanish, I managed to make myself understood. All of a sudden, I realized I had a natural attitude for communicating and in that moment I became even more aware of my vocation: I wanted to teach everyone how to make pizza. I wasn't the only one who noticed my talent. In fact, Donato invited me to take part in his stall during a very important exhibition of the sector attended by the most important chefs

Davide and Donato De Santis during the recording of the program

of South America. After a few months, the locals began to recognize me on the street after having watched the episode of the tv-show 'Pizza alla Donato'.

I got invited to another tv show 'Tu vida mas simple', presented by chef Narda Lopes. That was the moment I began to really feel passionate about this mode of communication. My relationship with the camera was born in that exact moment and – believe me – never ever would I have thought that this aspect was to become so important in my life.

The trip to Argentina was also a perfect chance to meet Pedro Picciau, a famous Italian-Argentinian chef I had once met in Capri, along with Donato, as well as the father of a dear friend of mine, Luciano. Pedro had won the fresh pasta championship that took place in Italy many years before: he was a master of pasta dough and a man of infinite wisdom. My best friends Luciano, Mariano and Veronica hosted me for a long time, allowing me to experience those lands just like a local. I remember those days so well, sipping wine and enjoying an incomparable *asado* all together.

Argentina gifted me with indescribable emotions and allowed me to meet incredible people such as Donato and Pedro, who grew fond of me. They used to call me *el Pibe* – the young boy – having tracked my professional advancement as well as my personal growth. They have never stopped believing in me and still today I am in touch with them: I am happy to admit Argentina gave me a family to rely on. The experience in that far away land also made me aware of my strong points, that is to say, my communicative power, the technical knowledge of the matter and a strong inclination for internationalizing my job.

Therefore, even though unconsciously, a longing for a quality improvement as a professional pulled at me. But I was still too young and decided not to listen to that hidden need and to follow the good old road.

Around Italy and the world with Rossopomodoro

I came back to Italy and was looking for a job near home, in Casoria. At the time I started dealing with a new format of pizza – it was the first time for my *pizza al metro*, a constructive and very fun experience. However, once again, I felt that this type of pizza was still not the final goal for me to reach. One day I received a phone call from Antonio Bastelli, from

Davide at the opening of Rossopomodoro at Eataly Chicago

Rossopomodoro, who informed me about a great opportunity at Pizze e Contorni, in Fuorigrotta, another restaurant by Rossopomodoro that was looking for a head pizzaiolo.

I felt the need to move from Casoria because living in a livelier neighborhood such as Fuorigrotta would have certainly done me some good. Pizze e Contorni had adopted an innovative concept of pizzeria, offering the chance to taste the traditional classic Neapolitan pizza, now from a modern perspective: in fact, the client had the opportunity to choose the diameter of the

Davide during the opening of Rossopomodoro at Eataly New York with Gwyneth Paltrow

pizza, and whether to pair it with cooked dishes, selecting among all the preferred side dishes, matched with any sort of base, that could be served both directly on top of the pizza, or as a separate dish.

Today the pizzeria is still located in Via Giulio Cesare, a few hundred meters away from the University of Naples. Every single day dozens and dozens of students flooded into the pizzeria and that lively place kept me there for 3 long years.

After that highly intense period, I received a phone call from Salvatore Mugnano, head pizzaiolo in Rossopomodoro who – at that time – was opening several pizzerias all around Italy.

"Would you like to come to Milan?" he asked, and then he added: "Should it not be Milan, where would you like to go then?"

At the time my brother Francesco was living

and working in Bologna, and so I chose the county town of Emilia Romagna as my next destination.

In fact, it proved to be a valid base for what was about to happen next. From Bologna, during those years, I moved all across the Italian boot: I was involved in openings in Pavia, Milan, Parma, Catania, Trieste, etc.

Rossopomodoro decided to gather an opening team that would have inaugurated all the pizzerias that were about to open all around the world. I was thus named head pizzaiolo of this new crew, under the supervision of Salvatore Mugnano. To complete the team Alessandro Pilla in direction, Ciro Sorrentino first and then Bartolo Russo. Together we opened more than 90 venues all around the world. How exciting were the openings in Tokyo, Istanbul, München, Copenhagen and –

above all – New York! Indeed, at 23 years old the image of the man and professional I'd wanted to be began to take shape in my mind and in my heart: a pizzaiolo with classical roots and a modern, international entrepreneurial spirit. Above all, I understood that I loved to relate in a direct way with all my clients and customers. It was so stimulating to be in contact with the public – it made me feel alive. I knew I wanted to communicate, teach and spread, by any means, the word of Neapolitan pizza all around the world.

Salvatore Mugnano told me that we would be opening a venue in New York. For the first time – I must admit – I felt so scared to go overseas, pursuing the American Dream. Let's tell the truth, who among us had never dreamt of it at least once in their lives?

I was so scared – true but, at the same time, I was 26 years old and so, oblivious of everything, I finally decided to go to America. I arrived in New York in August 2010. It was evening. I took a taxi and asked to be taken to Rossopomodoro in Eataly's Flatiron restaurant on Fifth Avenue. I had lived in America for two and a half years and during this time I understood how I wanted to live my life: travelling and making pizzas all around

the world. In New York I had the chance to learn English as well as to cook for Jay Z, Beyoncé, Gwyneth Paltrow and other stars of the show business. I had money in my pockets, a nice apartment in Manhattan and a craving for life. Moreover, the restaurant used to register amazing numbers and we didn't lack work for sure.

I felt so pleased. Starting from New York, I went on opening Rossopomodoro's pizzerias all around the States. I first moved to Chicago, then Boston, Las Vegas, even Brazil and so on and so forth: I was living the dream!

World Championship of Pizzaiuoli and the first encounter with Mulino Caputo

I came back to Italy around mid-2012 but it was only in September 2013 that my life took a turning point: I won the world championship of pizza makers that, by complete chance, happened to occur that year in Naples. After 7 years, I managed to bring the Caputo Trophy back to the Neapolitan city, the cradle of a philosophy that – over the past years – I had learnt to practice. It was the twelfth edition and that year more than 300 pizzaioli from all over the world took part in the competition, each with their own style, each with their certainties and insecurities. It was a memorable moment. From that day on, I decided to follow the path that destiny had traced for me. However, I couldn't have done it without the help of Mulino Caputo, that has always supported me and believed in me. Since the very beginning.

Not only did I want to make pizza, I wanted to show people how to do it.

Thanks to the business of Antimo Caputo I widened my range of action all around the world. In fact, I had the chance to confront

Davide is awarded by Carmine Caputo at World Championship of Pizzaiuoli

diverse cultures that have enriched me both from a professional and human point of view.

I had finally reached the internationalization and technical knowledge that allowed my career to finally make that huge improvement in quality. In fact, thanks to Mulino Caputo I had the opportunity to deepen the technical and scientific knowledge related to flours that, as you will have the chance to read further on, is the base of those techniques for pizza manufacturing.

I finally managed to implement my communicative talent and began to travel all around the world – far and wide, in more than 140 restaurants, teaching the verb of Neapolitan pizza to schools for foreign pizzaioli. I was able to render even the most complicated concepts in a much easier way, as well as to impart specific techniques using different languages, addressing the most disparate people of the world: Chinese, Thai, Brazilian, Scandinavian... It didn't cause me any stress at all, because I was happy to teach other pizzaioli the basic rules and principles to make an excellent pizza.

So, to date, 80% of my time has been dedicated to this cause, thanks to Mulino Caputo and Rossopomodoro. I owe them a lot and truly hope to have fully returned all of the trust they put on me over these years.

From pizzeria to homemade pizza

I have therefore laid the foundations for living the life I have always craved for. It all began many years ago, when I used to run round and round with that very large t-shirt at the Da Gennaro pizzeria in Naples, meaning, living on pizza.

Nevertheless, I have always been a person who has never set any limit to his own human growth and, after all the professional success, a new need began to arise, evoked by the fact

that many people, among whom friends and relatives, day after day, were asking me recipes and pieces of advice to make a good homemade pizza. And so – as it usually happens – a bit for fun and a bit out of need, I began to take advantage of the new technologies and social networks to do something that I already did as a job: recording pizza video-recipes. Never ever would I have thought to achieve such resounding success. The uploaded videos were quite rustic, not professional at all, and maybe it was for this exact reason that they could reach users with no frills, nor fables.

With Mulino Caputo and ItaliaSquisita I then posted a video on YouTube that, to date – and I can hardly believe it – is the most visualized video related to Neapolitan pizza, made in Italy, in the whole world. An historical goal.

In that very moment I added another brick to my life, communication and multimedia divulgation – that has received a vigorous push thanks to the work and advice from ItaliaSquisita. The video – the first one ever dedicated to homemade pizza made by a professional pizzaiolo – represents me using that precise technique I had learnt earlier on, whilst in Argentina: the refractory stone. I understood that, in my life, nothing happens by chance.

Thanks to my videos I now understand that the generational passage of family recipe books does not exist anymore as each and everybody prefers looking for all sorts of online info when thinking about making a new dish. However, sometimes we do not realize that experience and credibility are two key values, not so easy to find, and never to be left behind.

Therefore I decided to write this book so that one day, not that far after all, anyone in the world would be able to find truthful recipes, so as to transmit all the love that one holds inside through the making of an authentic and tasty homemade pizza.

This is a book about pizza and, just after the love I feel for my dear ones, it is for sure what makes me the happiest. I will recount

Davide in Dubai at Diego Armando Maradona's home

techniques and recipes, as if they were roads to lead you towards happiness.

Each type of pizza dough will be matched with explanations and tips that will guide you step by step towards the realization of a pizza that is truly yours. All the recipes are entirely created to be made at home. Soon after you get started, you will notice that making pizza can be a form of entertainment and, above all, a genuine form of nutrition and sharing, that in some cases – I am afraid – we are still missing.

Many people asked what is the secret to making a good homemade pizza. There is no secret, but three elements that will certainly happen to be useful: heart, hands and mind. Love is the glue that sticks everything together and allows us to give all of ourselves to others. Because cuisine is a science, so full of love. Thanks to our solid and rock-hard tradition, I foresee a bright

future for Neapolitan pizza that, also thanks to our contribution, has grown massively over the last few years. At this point it is possible to eat a good pizza even abroad, from China to Australia. The speed of information and the will not to settle for the first recipe you bump into will certainly make the difference. Pizza is love and love is good for everyone and everyone should be able to spread it in the most efficient way.

This book is not addressed to my colleagues, but to all those people who love cooking and cannot do without bringing a great pizza to the table, at least once a week.

Welcome into my world. Welcome into the world of pizza.

Neapolitan PIZZA

Production Procedural Guidelines

Neapolitan pizza is a symbolic gastronomic product of Italy in the world. Let's start from tradition and then explore all the possible variations for homemade pizza.

According to the Production Procedural Guidelines of the *Pizza Napoletana* Traditional Specialty Guaranteed, inserted in the Official Gazette of the Italian Republic in 2010, general series – n.56, Neapolitan Pizza officially appears between 1715 and 1725. In many historical documents, pizza is mentioned as a culinary specialty of Naples. The writer Franco Salerno even defines it as one of the greatest Neapolitan gastronomic inventions.

As early as 1700, Naples began to fill up with small shops, called 'pizzerias', specializing in Neapolitan pizza. The success of pizza also reached the king of Naples, Ferdinando di Borbone, who even broke the court etiquette and went to eat it in one of the most famous pizzerias in the city.

So, at the time, pizzerias became a trendy place.

The most popular pizzas were the Marinara (created in 1734) and the Margherita (created between 1796 and 1810) which was offered to the Queen of Italy in 1889 on the occasion of her visit to Naples, precisely because its colors recall the Italian flag.

In a very short time, the fame of pizza crossed the borders of the city and, soon, of all of Italy. Pizzerias were coming to light everywhere and in May 1984, the old Neapolitan pizza makers drew up a certification of production, registered with an official deed by the notary Antonio Carannante from Naples, a first step to safeguard a product that made Naples and its history famous.

Dough

The admitted ingredients:
→ Wheat flour
→ Brewer's yeast
→ Still drinking water
→ Peeled tomatoes
  (and/or fresh cherry tomatoes)
→ Sea salt (or cooking salt)
→ EVO oil

→ Garlic
→ Oregano
→ Basil
→ PDO buffalo mozzarella
  from Campania
→ Mozzarella TSG

Preparation

Add 1 liter of water and salt (the quantity must be between 50 and 55 g) into a stand mixer, then add 180 g of flour and 3 g of the brewer's yeast. Start the mixer using a dough-hook and gradually add up to a maximum of 1800 g of W 220-380 flour (from 50% to 55% of hydration). According to the procedural guidelines this first step requires approximately 10 minutes.

Then continue with the processing of the dough in the machine for 20 minutes at low speed. The final dough must be elastic, soft and non-sticky.

Rising process

The procedural guidelines divide the rising process into two phases.

The first step involves transferring the dough from the machine to the counter of the pizzeria. The dough is left to rest for 2 hours covered with a damp cloth to prevent it from drying out. After 2 hours, the pizza maker can proceed with the cutting of the dought balls which must weigh between 180 and 250 g.

During the second phase, the balls are placed in food boxes and stored at 18-22°C for a minimum of 4 hours and a maximum of 6 hours.

Stretching

Remove the dough from the rising box with a spatula and place it on the surface of the counter sprinkled with flour. Stretch out the pizza by pressing it with your fingertips, moving from the center outwards, and turning over the dough several times.

→ The art of the Neapolitan Pizzaiuolo
has been recognized by UNESCO as
an intangible heritage of humanity in 2017

The disc must not exceed 35 cm in diameter, the center must not be thicker than 0.4 cm (tolerance of ± 10%) and the cornicione (border) must not exceed 1-2 cm in height.

The procedural guidelines do not admit a diverse method of stretching out pizza than the one performed by hand directly by the pizza maker.

Topping

The procedural guidelines describe the ingredients, the respective quantities and the methods for adding the topping:

Marinara pizza
→ 70-100 g of crushed peeled tomatoes which must be spread with a spoon over the entire surface of the pizza following a spiral motion.
→ A pinch of salt and a pinch of oregano should be spread over the whole base following a spiral motion.
→ 1 garlic clove, peeled and cut into slices, sprinkled on the pizza.
→ 4-5 g of EVO oil (tolerance of ± 20%) sprinkled with a beak-spouted oil jug following a spiral motion.

Margherita pizza with PDO buffalo mozzarella from Campania or with Mozzarella TSG
→ 60-80 g of crushed peeled tomatoes which must be spread with a spoon over the entire surface of the pizza following a concentric spiral motion.
→ A pinch of salt.
→ 80-100 g PDO buffalo mozzarella from Campania or Mozzarella TSG.
→ A few fresh basil leaves.
→ 4-5 g of EVO oil (tolerance of ± 20%) sprinkled with a beak-spouted oil jug following a concentric spiral motion.

Baking

The procedural guidelines only allow baking in a wood oven at 485°C and baking times must not exceed 60-90 seconds. After the baking process, the pizza maker must plate the pizza, to be served and consumed immediately in the place of production.

Neapolitan pizza is characterized by a thick and golden cornicione (meaning the border), it must be elastic and it must be easily foldable.

Homemade Neapolitan

PIZZA

In this Masterclass I will guide you step by step and I will reveal all the secrets for a homemade Neapolitan pizza baked on refractory stone that does not fear any comparison with the pizzerias. It would almost feel like we are making pizza together!

I've always been wondering how to make traditional Neapolitan pizza in a domestic oven. Very frequently homemade pizzas don't even remotely resemble the ones made in a pizzeria and people who make them feel frustrated and incompetent. The reality is that there are objective limitations that make it so difficult to achieve comparable results. It's not about being a professionals or an amateurs, it is a matter of tools, tricks and processes.

I then analyzed the substantial differences and tried to understand the best solutions adoptable. The biggest difference is the temperature of the oven.

A professional wood oven reaches a temperature between 380 and 450°C without delays, allowing you to cook a pizza in 90 seconds only. Whilst a domestic oven reaches on average temperatures ranging between 220 and 250°C (the latest generation ovens can reach 300°C, which are in any case below the 450°C of wood-burning ovens (→ p.172 Ovens).

To make up for and bridge the temperature gap, I tried to apply a cooking technique that Argentinians use extensively, both for cooking meat and to keep food warm: a stone heated directly on the embers. Why not give it a try?

I had a thin refractory stone made of such size suitable for the domestic oven (perhaps I was the first in Italy to experiment this technique for pizza).

I experimented a lot, and the results were never satisfying. The pizza tended to get too dry and toasted, and for a professional like me, always attentive to quality, it became a real challenge. So I did the unthinkable: I added ingredients to the ones belonging to the traditional recipe and, proceeding by trial and error, I achieved results that I didn't even envision. Follow me and trust my suggestions, you will be amazed too!

Work tools	For the preparation	For the cooking
	→ Large wooden (madia) or plastic container (preferably rectangular)	→ Domestic oven
		→ Refractory stone
	→ Work surface for kneading (preferably made of wood or marble)	→ Wooden peel to slide the pizza from the work surface to the refractory stone
	→ Scraper or plastic spatula	
	→ Containers for ingredients	
	→ Container with lid for leavening	
	→ Kitchen scale	

Homemade Neapolitan pizza Masterclass

Dough

4–6 pizzas
500 ml water
800 g 0 or 00 medium strength flour
25 g salt
1 g active dry yeast (or 2 g of fresh brewer's yeast)
10 g sugar
25 g EVO oil

1 Start adding 3/4 of the flour in the madia (or in a plastic container) trying to take up only half of the available space.

2 Add the yeast to the flour. Dissolving the yeast into water, a common practice at home, can compromise the leavening because if too cold it might inactivate the yeast.

3 Then pour the water into the empty half of the madia and dissolve the salt into it, then add the sugar.

4 Start mixing the ingredients slowly, dissolving the flour in the water so as to avoid lumps.

5 Once you have reached a good consistency of the dough, proceed by kneading more vigorously with movements from the bottom up. This allows the gluten to develop and create the gluten mesh.

6 Then pour the EVO oil gradually and work in the madia until the oil is completely absorbed.

Calculating the ideal temperature of the water when making the dough

Water is a fundamental ingredient in all kind of doughs and its temperature can also influence and affect the success of the final product. Therefore, it is important to know that the final temperature of the dough must range between 20 and 24°C. It should never exceed 27°C, otherwise the gluten begins to yield and the dough (in this case the loaves) will develop in width and not in height, resulting in a less strength dough, making it less workable.

To calculate the ideal temperature of the water, we can use a simple formula.

The temperature we wish the dough to achieve is multiplied by 3. The room temperature, that of the flour and that of the machine or hands are subtracted from this figure.

If you want to make the dough in a stand mixer, it is important to know that machines discharge at medium from 3 to 15 degrees at an average speed and therefore, by convention, the reference value is 10°C. To give a practical example, if we want a dough at 20°C, the room temperature is 20°C, the temperature of the flour is 19°C (because it is usually one degree lower than the room one), and the machine temperature is 10°C the calculation will be as follows:

$$20 \times 3 = 60$$
$$60 - 20 - 19 - 10 = 11°C$$

The water to be used for the dough must be at a temperature of 11°C. In summer this calculation could give negative results.

Therefore, by convention, water is used between 2 and 4°C degrees.

→ If the wooden madia (the container used for the dough) is new, I recommend making a light batter with water and flour and passing it through all corners and edges to seal the joints and prevent water from leaking

→ If you want to use fresh brewer's yeast just double the dose indicated for the dry yeast

4

→ Using oil in a homemade pizza dough helps to obtain a product with a texture between crunchy and soft. On the other hand, sugar helps to give color without significantly affecting the leavening

→ The fats in the dough are always added at the end so as not to compromise the absorbing power of the fibers

6

7

7 Wash your hands with flour and transfer the dough onto a work surface well dusted with flour. Add the rest of the flour and start kneading vigorously with both hands, applying pressure only with your palm and never with your fingers so as to avoid tearing it.

8 Drag the dough forward using the weight of the body and then bring it back. Continue in this way, working vigorously and being careful not to tear the dough.

9 The handmade dough must be worked for about 15-20 minutes. This allows the dough to develop the gluten mesh for optimal leavening and cooking.

10 Then form a single round dough. At this stage it is essential to touch and manipulate the dough gently, almost caressing it.

11 Clean the madia from any lump and flour residues and transfer the dough into it. Seal with a lid and let it rise at 18-22°C for about 40 minutes.

Mixing with a machine

If you have a mixer available, making homemade pizza dough will be faster and less tiring. Just add the ingredients in the same order used for the handmade dough and knead at a medium speed for about 10 minutes. The disadvantage of using a machine mainly concerns capacity: the stand mixers for domestic use usually allow you to make doughs of up to 1 kg. It is advisable to check the maximum quantity of flour before starting to knead in order to avoid compromising its functioning.

→ To make the dough I prefer using the wooden madia because it starts absorbing excess moisture from the first resting

11

Cutting phase

12 After 40 minutes, take the dough (try not to crush it in order to avoid breaking the air bubbles that have developed) and place it back onto the work surface. Divide the dough into pieces of the same size and create dough balls. Then form balls of dough of more or less the same weight: usually for a pizza of 28-32 cm in diameter you need 230-250 g of dough.

First method

Remove the pieces of dough from the loaf with your hands (or a spatula), seal the lower end with your fingers so as not to open the dough, then place the ball onto the work surface and round it between the palm of your hand and the work surface so as to create a smooth ball.

This is the method I prefer, I learned it as a young boy in Porta Capuana and, in the cutting phase, I instinctively use it!

Second method

Lift the loaf with both hands, push the dough inwards with your right hand and then 'squeeze' it. This method is very similar to the process called 'mozzatura' and used when making mozzarella.

Third method

Cut a piece of dough from the loaf and work it with the palms of your hands until it is rounded.

First method

Second method

Third method

Rising and stretching

13 Transfer the balls into a wooden or plastic container, cover and leave to rise for at least 6-12 hours at 18-22°C. Once the rising time has passed, the balls will have doubled in volume and will be ready for stretching.

14 Take a loaf of dough from the leavening box by carefully separating the edges from the walls and lifting it from underneath with the help of a spatula to avoid deflating it.

15 Transfer it onto a working surface dusted with flour and start spreading it by gently pressing your fingertips in the center of the dough. Continue by stretching the center of the dough from the inside outwards in order to leave the borders thicker.

16 Keeping your hands always well floured, spread the pizza: hold the disc of dough still with one hand and, with the other hand, gently stretch the disc outwards, being careful not to tear the dough.

17 Once you have obtained a pizza base of the desired size, proceed with the topping.

13

→ The secret to stretching out a good pizza is to work it as little as possible

→ It is important not to overly widen and stretch the disc of dough as you run the risk of piercing it during the topping phase

Topping

1 pizza
80 g peeled tomatoes
80 g fiordilatte mozzarella
EVO oil to taste
Grated Parmigiano cheese to taste (or pecorino)
Basil to taste
Salt to taste

18 Spread the tomato on the pizza base evenly, leaving the border free.

19 Then sprinkle with the fiordilatte cut into strips, a few basil leaves and grated Parmigiano Reggiano. Top with a drizzle of EVO oil (the classic 6 shape for pizza chefs) and bake.

Mozzarella cheese

Fiordilatte mozzarella must always be cut with a knife (electrical machines indeed separate the dough from the liquid) and in medium-sized strips: if too small it dehydrates quickly and risks burning during cooking, if too large you might end up having too much water on the pizza base, compromising the cooking and the taste, too. If you want to use PDO buffalo mozzarella from Campania, it is recommended to cut it in advance and let it drain on a colander in order to remove any excess.

Tomato

Tomato is a fundamental ingredient for pizza makers. Tradition calls for San Marzano, but there are different varieties and each pizza chef has his favorite. Peeled tomatoes can be processed using the traditional method (crushed by hand with your fingers in order to obtain different consistencies) or with a vegetable mill. It is absolutely not recommended to blend the tomato: it loses its consistency, becomes very watery and evaporates during cooking, this will make the pizza dry and not very tasty. Furthermore, for the Neapolitan pizza the tomato is always used raw and never cooked. You can use cooked sauces as a condiment, but not for a traditional margherita.

To season the tomato
1 g salt per 100 g tomato
1 drizzle of EVO oil to give it shininess and flavor

→ Don't overdo the tomato, otherwise the pizza won't cook and the base will stay too moist

→ If your oven does not reach very high temperatures, I recommend adding mozzarella on the pizza after 3 minutes from the start of the baking to prevent it from burning

→ The static mode is the most constant and easiest to manage, but a lot depends on your oven and yourself

18   19

Baking

The oven must be preheated to at a high temperature (→ **p.178 Domestic ovens**). The refractory stone must be placed in the oven as you turn it on to make sure that it has reached its temperature when the pizza is placed in the oven. Using a peel lightly dusted with flour, transfer the pizza from the counter to the oven. In this phase, it is essential that your movements are firm but delicate. Once in the oven, tilt the peel on the refractory stone and with soft movements slide the pizza directly in contact with the stone. Bake for about 5-7 minutes, until the cornicione (border) is swollen and golden.

It is advisable to turn the pizza at least once or twice to obtain uniform cooking.

Variants

Pizza doesn't have to be a taboo, everyone is free to experiment and choose the one that best suits their taste. By using the same recipe and changing only the flours or part of the procedure you can obtain products that differ from the traditional Neapolitan pizza.

Whole wheat

Ingredients
500 g water
25 g salt
800 kg whole wheat flour
1 g active dry yeast
(or 2 g fresh brewer's yeast)
50 g EVO oil
10 g sugar

Preparation
Mix the ingredients with the same procedure as the Neapolitan pizza, stretching and baking are the same.

With cereals

Ingredients
500 g cold water
650 g 0 or 00 medium strength flour
150 g multi-grain flour
25 g salt
1 g active dry yeast
(or 2 g fresh brewer's yeast)
50 g EVO oil

Preparation
Mix the ingredients with the same procedure as the Neapolitan pizza, stretching and baking are the same.

Long leavening

Ingredients
500 g water
800 g 0 flour or 00 strong flour
25 g salt
1 g active dry yeast
(or 2 g fresh brewer's yeast)
25 g EVO oil
10 g sugar

Preparation
Mix the ingredients and allow them to rise in mass in a closed container or in a wooden container for 12 hours at 18-22°C. Cut the balls out and allow them to rise for 12 more hours at 18-22°C. The stretching and baking techniques are the same as those used for the traditional Neapolitan pizza.

Neapolitan pizza cooked in a pan

◍ The dough and the methods of preparation are the same as for the Neapolitan pizza in the domestic oven, cooking involves the combination of a pan and a oven. You can apply this kind of cooking only if you have a traditional gas burner due to the fact that electric or induction stoves do not guarantee the same results. Cooking in a pan is a useful solution, not only for those who have ovens that do not reach high temperatures. It is a valid alternative for everyone, as it shortens the cooking time of the pizza.

Turn the oven on at maximum temperature and set it to grill mode. Meanwhile, heat a non-stick pan over a medium flame.

Roll the pizza out using the same method as for the Neapolitan one and transfer it to the pan. Add the topping directly in the pan, maintaining the same doses and following the same steps as for the Neapolitan pizza baked in a domestic oven.

Cook in a pan with a lid on a medium flame for about 2 minutes, then finish it in the oven for other 2 minutes.

→ For this type of cooking, a pan with no plastic or wooden elements must be employed, so that it can also be used in the oven

Vesuvio Calzone

For the filling

150 g ricotta
100 g fiordilatte
(or smoked provola)
80 g Neapolitan
cracklings
10 g peeled tomatoes
10 g pecorino from
Bagnoli
Milk to taste
EVO oil to taste
Basil to taste
Black pepper to taste

1 calzone

◍ For this type of calzone you need a full 250 g loaf
and another 130 g loaf as a cover, the dough is the same
as for the homemade Neapolitan pizza.

Start by cutting the cracklings into cubes, then dilute the
ricotta a little (if it is too dry, you can add a little milk to make
it silkier and easier to stretch). Cut the fiordilatte into cubes
(not into strips as you would do for a pizza, in order
to facilitate the evaporation of liquids).
    Then stretch out the first loaf: unlike pizza, to make
calzone, the edges must be thin and the center (where the
filling is placed) thicker, so that it does not get wet and does
not break during cooking. The edge of the two discs must be
thin because, once the calzone is closed, there is a risk of not
baking it well or that the edge becomes too 'bready'.
    Add the ingredients in this order: ricotta, cracklings,
mozzarella, black pepper, basil shredded with your hands
and a drizzle of EVO oil.
    Stretch out the second loaf without working it too much
(just stretch it a little with your hands) and cover the filling,
being careful to seal all the edges well.

Sprinkle the surface with tomato (not too much, otherwise the calzone will stay raw), add some grated pecorino cheese and a drizzle of EVO oil. Bake on a refractory stone in a preheated oven at 230°C for 5-7 minutes. Take it out from the oven and add some grated pecorino cheese and a drizzle of EVO oil.

→ If you do not want an excessively swollen calzone, just pierce the upper part slightly. You can also add some topping on it, as you wish. The result will be a pizza on the outside and a calzone on the inside

Variants

The Vesuvio-shaped calzone is undoubtedly the most spectacular
to serve to your beloved ones, but if you want to keep surprising them,
here are further possible traditional techniques.

Classic calzone

To make a classic calzone use a single 250 g ball. It is stretched in the same way as a Vesuvio calzone, it is stuffed by placing the filling on one half of the disc only and it is then closed by folding the half with no filling onto the other one, giving it the classic crescent shape being careful to seal the edges well as to prevent the filling from leaking during the cooking process. Before cooking, a light pressure is applied to the top side in order to better spread the filling inside.

Half pizza half ripieno (stuffed)

To make this type of pizza you need a 250 g loaf and a mixed stretching technique. One half is shaped as a classic Neapolitan pizza cornicione, meaning by pushing from the inside outwards to obtain a thicker border and a thinner center. The second half, on the other hand, is stretched by following the technique used for the calzone.

On the calzone side, the condiment is placed on the base, in the center of the half and the dough is folded over like a calzone. The half pizza, instead, is seasoned as explained in the masterclass.

Deep-fried pizza

For the filling
500 g ricotta
500 g smoked provola
300 g pork cracklings
(typical pressed meat
from Naples)
Black pepper to taste
Milk to taste
300 g peeled tomatoes
(optional)
Basil to taste (optional)
Frying oil as needed

1 pizza

◍ The procedure for the dough is the same as the one used to making homemade Neapolitan pizza, the substantial difference is in the cooking method and for this reason we will avoid adding any sugar and oil to the dough.

The difference is also in the size of the dough balls: if you want to make a round deep-fried pizza, they must be about 100-120 g each (you will need 2 to make one pizza), whilst if you want to make the classic *pescitiello* or *battilocchio* pizza, that is, with an elongated and not round shape, use a single 250 g loaf.

Cut the cracklings and provola into small cubes so as to prevent it from releasing too much water during the cooking process and, separately, work the ricotta with a little milk to make it creamier. If you decide to use tomato, season it (1 g salt per 100 g tomato) and mash it with your hands.

For the round deep-fried pizza tretch out both balls, using the same technique of the Vesuvio calzone. Indeed, you start from the border, which must be thinner than the center. The center will stay thicker in order to hold the filling without breaking during cooking.

On the other hand, the boarder must be thin to avoid that, given the overlapping of the two balls, it becomes too thick and bready.

→ The round deep-fried pizza is more suitable to be served and eaten on the plate. On the other hand, should the idea be to eat while standing up, I recommend making a *battilocchio* deep-fried pizza

To make a *battilocchio* deep-fried pizza (one 250 g dough loaf),
stretch out the dough out with the same logic as for the round
deep-fried pizza: keep the edge thin and the center thicker.
Once stretched, fill it and seal it like a classic calzone.

Place the ricotta on the base, then add the cracklings,
provola, ground black pepper and, if you like, a spoonful
of tomato and a few basil leaves.

In order to make a round pizza, seal it by placing the
second loaf on top. For the *battilocchio* one instead, fold it
in half as if it were a half moon. In both cases, the borders
must be tightly sealed in order in order to prevent the filling
from leaking during the cooking process. Fry in a low, large
pan in pre-heated oil at 180°C. Once the pizza is swollen and
golden, drain and pat-dry the excess oil.

Gluten free Neapolitan PIZZA

Until a few years ago, eating a good gluten free pizza was unthinkable. In recent years, companies and professionals started experimenting with flours, blends and processing techniques, achieving excellent results. In this section I will explain how to create a gluten free Neapolitan pizza at home!

Gluten free Neapolitan pizza Masterclass

Kneading and cutting

4–6 pizzas
1 kg gluten free flour
10 g dry active yeast
700 g water
30 g salt
50 g EVO oil

1 Add the flour in the mixer bowl, the yeast and run the machine at medium speed. Pour in the water gradually, then add salt.

2 Stop the machine and carefully remove the dough from the edges using a plastic spatula. Work for another 2 minutes.

3 Scrape any residual dough off the edges of the bowl again, add the EVO oil and knead for 3 more minutes. The total working time will not exceed 7 minutes.

4 Using your hands greased with EVO oil, create dough balls by cutting portions of dough of the same weight (from 250 to 300 g) directly from the bowl of the mixer.

5 Cover them securely with cling film and leave to rest in the refrigerator for at least 4-6 hours.

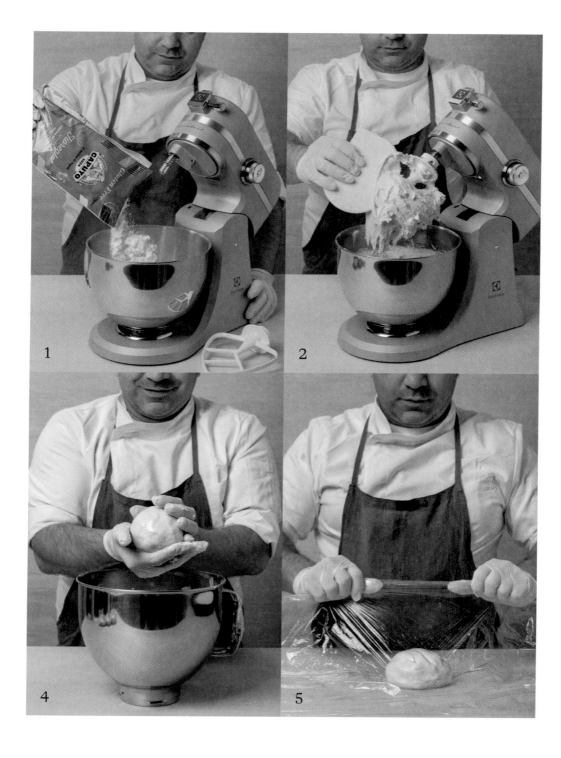

Stretching

6 Once the raising time has passed, take a loaf, remove the cling film and toss it in the rice flour to prevent the dough from sticking to the counter.

7 Spread the dough evenly, gently stretching the center and keeping the edged slightly thicker.

8 Once the stretching is completed, grease the surface with a drizzle of EVO oil: this will guarantee a more golden and less pale pizza.

→ In order not to break the dough when sliding it into the oven, it is advisable to stretch it directly on the wooden peel

→ Use a plastic spatula to compact the edges and give the right shape

Topping

80 g of peeled tomatoes
80 g fiordilatte mozzarella
EVO oil to taste
Grated Parmigiano cheese to taste (optional)
Basil to taste
Salt to taste

9 For the procedure concerning the topping ingredients of the gluten free Neapolitan pizza (→ **p.40 Homemade Neapolitan pizza**).

10 Bake on refractory stone in a preheated oven at 230°C for 5-7 minutes.

Gluten free deep-fried pizza

1 tablespoon of tomato sauce (cooked with oil and garlic)
60 g buffalo ricotta
Grated Parmigiano to taste
Basil to taste

Frying oil to taste

1 deep-fried pizza

⑪ Using the same dough of the gluten free Neapolitan pizza, it is possible to make the so-called montanara deep-fried pizza: not stuffed, but flavored after frying.

Stretch out the dough on a sheet of baking paper and make small holes with your fingers over the entire surface. In a pan large enought to contain a pizza bring the frying oil to 180°C.
   Keeping the baking paper in place, immerse the dough – previously stretched – into the pan, it will come off easily after a few seconds of cooking. Once cooked and golden brown, drain the pizza and pat-dry the excess oil with absorbent paper.
   Season with a spoonful of warm tomato sauce, dots of ricotta, some grated Parmigiano cheese and a few basil leaves.

→ The gluten free dough must be kneaded for no more than 7 minutes. Mixing it longer than necessary will overheat it and compromise the leavening

→ Working the dough with gloves and covering the dough with cling film will prevent food contamination

→ The gluten free dough can be stored in the refrigerator for up to 2 days

Contemporary

PIZZA

Among the new trends, contemporary Neapolitan pizza is certainly the most successful innovation. It is characterized by a very high cornicione (border) rich in air pockets, the hydration is higher and the rising times longer. At the base of these new styles of pizza, as it often happens, there are ancient methods. Let's discover them together!

Contemporary pizza masterclass

50% biga dough

4–6 pizzas

For the biga
500 g 0 or 00 strong flour
250 g water
5 g active dry yeast (or 10 g fresh brewer's yeast)

For the dough
All of the biga
500 g 0 or 00 weak flour
25 g salt
450 g water
5 g active dry yeast (or 10 g fresh brewer's yeast)
50 g EVO oil

For the biga

1 In a large bowl, mix all the ingredients together until you obtain a coarse mixture (the gluten net should not form).
Place in a container, cover with cling film and make small holes for the biga to breathe. Then allow to rest for 24 hours at a temperature of about 18-22°C.

For the dough

2 Transfer the biga into the machine using a dough hook, then add the rest of the flour and the yeast. If you want a product ready to be used in 3 hours, add 5 g of active dry yeast to the dough. If you have at least 8 hours for the rising, it is possible not to add the yeast and allow only the pre-ferment to work.

3 Start pouring half of the water in the kneading machine, let it work, add the salt, add the rest of the water gradually and drizzle the EVO oil in.

4 Work the dough for 15 minutes at medium speed until it becomes smooth and silky.

→ The use of the biga is recommended for those who want products with a greater rising: a very high and aerated border

→ The biga is a pre-dough technique that can be used for pizza but also for bread making

→ When you are using a pre-ferment, the kneading is called indirect

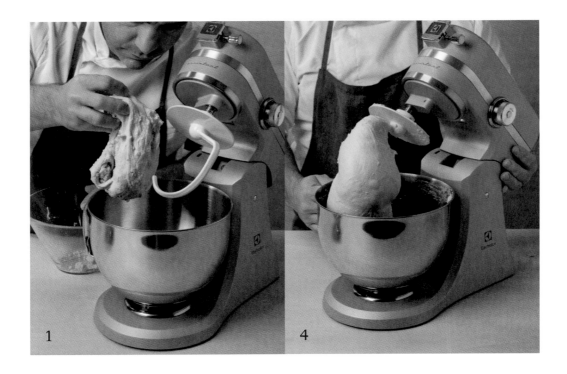

Rising and cutting

5 Allow the dough to rest in a sealed container for 40 minutes at a temperature of 18-22 °C.

6 Cut the dough into balls of about 280 g each and allow them to rise in a covered container at a temperature of 18-22°C for 6 to 8 hours until doubled in volume. If you prefer a longer rising in order to have an even more mature dough, you can place the balls in the refrigerator for 24 hours.

Stretching

7 The stretching of contemporary pizza differs from the one of Neapolitan pizza. In fact, the dough of the former is more hydrated. It must be treated more delicately in order to prevent it from releasing all the air accumulated during the rising process.

→ Being a dough with a higher hydration, it is recommended to sprinkle the working surface with semolina to prevent the dough from sticking to the surface. Even during the cooking process the semolina will allow us to obtain a more crunchy effect on the bottom

→ I recommend stretching it out on a wooden surface trying to push the air from the center towards the border in order to make it swell well when baking

→ Even the most hydrated dough of contemporary pizza is ideal for baking in the domestic oven

7

Seasoning and baking

1 pizza
80 g peeled tomatoes
80 g fiordilatte mozzarella
EVO oil to taste
Grated Parmigiano Reggiano to taste (optional)
Basil to taste
Salt to taste

For the procedure concerning the seasoning ingredients of contemporary Neapolitan pizza **(→ p.40 Homemade Neapolitan pizza)**.

Bake on a refractory stone in a preheated oven at 230°C for 5-7 minutes.

Poolish (or liquid biga)

For the poolish
500 g 0 or 00 medium
strength flour
500 g water
0.5 g active dry yeast
(or 1 g fresh brewer's
yeast)

For the dough
All the pre-ferment
200 g 0 or 00 weak flour
25 g salt
25 g EVO oil

4–6 pizzas

For the poolish
Mix the ingredients together until the mixture is smooth
and free of lumps. Store in a container covered with
a perforated cling film for 18-24 hours at 18-22°C.

For the dough
Mix the poolish with the flour, salt and EVO oil. Let it rest
in a sealed container at 18-22°C for about 1 hour. Cut the
dough balls out let it rise at 18-22°C in a covered container
for about 2-4 hours (the dough balls must double in volume).
Stretch out and bake the pizza following the directions
of the contemporary pizza with biga.

Poolish

The dose of yeast to make poolish varies according to the overall fermentation time of the liquid biga. The longer the leavening, the lower the quantity of yeast. The poolish must be prepared in advance, but it is good to calculate the right amount of yeast to use in relation to the hours of rest. The percentage of used yeast always refers to the total weight of the flour.

For a 2 hours rest, 3% of the yeast will be used on the total amount of flour. For 4 hours 1.5%; for 8 hours 0.75%; for 12 hours 0.2%; for 18 hours 0.1%.

→ Poolish is a technique that originates in cold countries and is particularly suitable for leavening during the cold seasons

→ The poolish gives the products a greater acidity, a characteristic that is very appreciated in bread making

Other indirect techniques

Autolysis

Ingredients
500 g 0 or 00 medium strength flour
275 ml water

Dough
5 g of active dry yeast
(or 10 g fresh brewer's yeast)
75 ml water
15 g salt
25 g oil

For 1 kg dough

it is a technique that takes advantage of the self-evolution of gluten.

The process is divided into three different phases.

First phase: autolytic dough
Gently knead the flour and the water required. If you use a stand mixer, you will need to use the dough hook and run the machine at minimum speed for about 5/8 minutes.

Second phase: rest
The resting time varies from 20 minutes to 24 hours.
The type of flour used basically determines the time: the greater the strength of the flour, the greater the resting time required.

For a pizza I would recommend not to exceed a 4 hours time first due to practical reasons. Also, because 30 minutes are sufficient.

Third phase: final kneading
We then proceed with the creation of the final dough by adding the rest of the ingredients, following the order and methods described above.

This technique brings several advantages.

The dough will have greater extensibility, will be more elastic and will also have a higher degree of water absorption. Autolytic doughs also guarantee products with a distinctive flavor, an excellent development and even a longer shelf life.

Pasta di riporto ('carryover dough')

In Naples, pasta di riporto is called *criscito*. This technique consists in using a natural leavening process which takes place thanks to the action of the rising of a previous dough.

In fact, the leftover Neapolitan pizza dough can be used as a base for a new dough the next day. The carryover dough

should be used at a minimum of 20% of the total weight of our dough (it is not necessary to add yeast, you can add a small amount of yeast as a starter to speed up the leavening).

Leavening times and procedures are the same as for homemade Neapolitan pizza.

Sheet pan

PIZZA

Pizza is not only the Neapolitan one served on the plate, pizza is a world full of variations that can satisfy everyone's tastes. In this section, I'll tell you about my sheet pan pizza: thick, soft and moist inside, and crunchy on the outside. There are many and very different recipes for sheet pan pizza and focaccia, this is my favorite!

Sheet pan baciata pizza Masterclass

Dough

1 tray 40x30cm

For biga (starting dough)
500 g 0 flour or 00 strong flour
250 g water
5 g active dry yeast (or 10 g fresh brewer's yeast)

For the dough
All of the biga
500 g 0 flour or 00 weak flour
25 g salt
550 g water
5 g dry active yeast
50 g EVO oil

For the biga
1 Mix all the ingredients together until you obtain a coarse compound (the gluten mesh must not form yet).

2 Place in a container, cover with cling film, make small holes to allow the biga to breathe and let it rest for 24 hours at around 18-22°C.
The biga can be worked by hand or in a machine at low speed.

For the dough
3 Place the biga into the machine with a dough hook and add the flour and yeast.

4 Pour a part of the water, allow it to work, add the salt, the rest of water and gradually the EVO oil.

5 Work the dough for 15 more minutes at medium speed until it is smooth, silky and elastic.

Rising and cutting

6 Let the dough rise in a sealed container at 18-22°C (about 18-22°C) until doubled in volume for at least 2 hours.

7 For a 30x40cm tray, cut out the dough into 600 g balls and let it rest in a well oiled container for 3-6 more hours.

Stretching

8 Turn the first ball over onto a wooden counter dusted with semolina, then start stretching the dough out with movements from top to bottom, starting from the center and returning back to the borders.

9 Place the first base into the pan and sprinkle the surface with EVO oil.

10 Repeat the same procedure for the second part of the dough and stretch it over the first base. Oil the surface again to obtain a more golden color.

→ To transfer the dough stretched out in the pan, you can help yourself by turning it over onto your arm and then gently place it in the pan to avoid tearing it or breaking the air bubbles

→ How to calculate the amount of dough for your pan: side × side × 0.5

→ The dough of this recipe will allow you to make a baciata as well a standard baking tray pizza

Baking

Place the pan on the base and bake in a preheated oven at maximum temperature for 15 minutes. Then move the baciata pizza to the center of the oven and bake for 15 more minutes. Remove from the oven, allow to cool slightly and stuff.

Stuffing

250 g mortadella
80 g rocket salad
250 g Shredded buffalo cheese

Gently remove the two focaccia halves and stuff by placing the rocket at the base, then the mortadella and finally the Shredded buffalo cheese.

Roman sheet pan pizza

You can make a classic pan pizza using the same dough. Just bake a single loaf of dough. If you want a thicker pizza, just add more dough, but pay attention to the baking time (the thicker the pizza, the longer time it takes). Finally, it is advisable to lower the temperature after the pizza has developed in the oven.

Gluten free sheet pan pizza

500 g gluten free flour
10 g active dry yeast
(or 20 g of fresh
brewer's yeast)
450 g water
15 g salt
25 g EVO oil

For the topping
Yellow cherry tomatoes
to taste
Red cherry tomatoes
to taste

EVO oil
Oregano to taste
Coarse salt to taste

1 tray 40×30 cm

Add the flour and yeast in the stand mixer with a flat beater and mix the two ingredients well. Add the water and let the machine work for about 3 minutes until the lumps of flour dissolve. Then add the salt and knead for 2 more minutes. Scrape the walls of the mixer bowl with a plastic spatula, add the EVO oil and allow it to work for another minute until the mixture is homogeneous. Place the dough directly into the pan (well oiled or greased with spray butter) and allow it to rise covered with cling film until doubled in volume (about 2 hours) at 18-22°C. Then create the classic focaccia holes by gently pressing your fingertips on the surface.

For the topping, cut the yellow and red tomatoes in half and press them lightly on the focaccia. Sprinkle the surface with a little oregano and coarse salt.

Bake in a preheated oven at 180°C for about 20 minutes, allow to cool before serving.

→ I recommend allowing the dough to rise directly in the tray that you will use for baking so as not to compromise the final result

A pizza maker's vocabulary

Punto di pasta · It is the moment when, by touching the dough, it becomes clear that it does no longer need any further ingredients because it is elastic, soft and well hydrated. From this moment on, the dough must rise and rest.

Incordatura · It is the procedure that, as you process the dough by machine or by hand, do so that the gluten net strengthens and structures itself. A dough that is 'incordato' is tenacious and elastic.

Wash your hands with flour · In the jargon of pizza makers we say 'we wash our hands with flour' to point to the action of cleaning our hands from the dough using flour and not water.

Stretch out 'a mezzo busto' (half-bust) • It means to stretch out the dough halfway and not entirely considering the fact that if stretched totally, you would not be able to slide the pizza from the counter to the peel.

Puntata • This is the name of the first rising of the dough.

Appretto • It is the phase in which the balls of pizza are left to rise after having cut them out.

Batocchi • An alternative way to call the loaves (or balls) of dough obtained after cutting the dough.

Martolelle • Before wood had been replaced by plastic, the batocchi were left to rise in wooden boxes called martolelle. Whilst the martola was the term used to identify the wooden container where the dough was made.

Alveoli (air pockets) • These are the typical bubbles that form in the dough as a consequence of the gas created during the rising. These are very evident in contemporary pizza.

Margherita with 4 tomatoes ◎ Red and yellow marinara ◎ Sausage and broccoli rabe ◎ Ham and mushrooms ◎ Nerano ◎ Oven fried pizza ◎ Calzone Scalorella

Traditional toppings

Toppings are an open book that must always be rewritten, where everyone can express their gastronomic imagination, even when it comes to tradition. Let yourself be inspired by seven of my variations on classic Neapolitan toppings.

Davide Civitiello HOMEMADE PIZZA

Margherita with 4 tomatoes

Recommended bases
→ p.29 Neapolitan
→ p.43 Whole wheat
→ p.52 Gluten free

For the first slice

50 g yellow datterini cherry tomatoes
30 g mozzarella fiordilatte
Black pepper to taste
Parmigiano Reggiano to taste

For the second slice

50 g pizzutello tomato
20 g grated pecorino from Bagnoli

For the third slice

50 g tomato San Marzano
30 g mozzarella fiordilatte

For the fourth slice

50 g red datterini cherry tomatoes
1 garlic clove
Oregano to taste

EVO oil to taste
Basil to taste

1 pizza

Stretch out the pizza and start filling as if it were 4 separate slices.

In the first quarter add the fiordilatte mozzarella cut into strips on the base, then add the yellow datterini cherry tomatoes cut in half and finish with a grind of black pepper.

Add the hand-pressed Pizzutello tomato on the base of the second slice and sprinkle with grated pecorino.

Then proceed with the topping of the third slice by adding the fiordilatte on the base and, on top, the tomato San Marzano cut into fillets.

Fill the last slice with halved red datterini cherry tomatoes, oregano and thin slices of garlic.

For the baking process

Bake the pizza in a preheated oven at 230°C (or at maximum power) on a refractory stone, and allow it to cook for about 5-7 minutes.

Finish the pizza with a drizzle of EVO oil, grated pecorino cheese on the slice with the pizzutello tomato and Parmigiano on the slice with yellow datterini cherry tomatoes.
Finally, add a few leaves of fresh basil to taste.

Davide Civitiello HOMEMADE PIZZA

Red and yellow marinara

Recommended bases
→ p.29 Neapolitan
→ p.43 Whole wheat
→ p.52 Gluten free

70 g yellow datterini
cherry tomatoes
70 g red datterini cherry
tomatoes
1 tablespoon of red
datterini cherry tomato
sauce
5 fillets of anchovies
from Cetara
5 g desalted capers
20 g black olives
from Gaeta
1 garlic clove
Oregano to taste
EVO oil to taste

1 pizza

Stretch out the pizza and, to prevent it from drying out
excessively, sprinkle the base with the datterini tomato sauce.
Then, add the yellow and red datterini cherry tomatoes cut
in half, the olives, a few slices of garlic, capers, oregano
and a drizzle of EVO oil.

For the baking process
Bake the pizza in a preheated oven at 230°C (or at maximum
power) on a refractory stone, and allow it to cook for about
5-7 minutes.

Add the anchovies after removing the pizza from the oven
and serve.

Davide Civitiello HOMEMADE PIZZA

Sausage and broccoli rabe

Recommended bases
→ p.29 Neapolitan
→ p.52 Gluten free

300 g broccoli rabe
(or 150 g cream
of broccoli rabe)
80 g Neapolitan sausage
120 g mozzarella
fiordilatte
20 g pecorino cheese
from Bagnoli
1 garlic clove
EVO oil to taste

1 pizza

Blanch the broccoli rabe, lightly sauté them in a pan with EVO oil and a clove of garlic, then blend them (after removing the garlic) until they reach a creamy texture.

Stretch out the dough and spread the cream on the base, chop the raw sausage on top, add the diced fiordilatte and a drizzle of EVO oil.

For the baking process
Bake the pizza in a preheated oven at 230°C (or at maximum power) on a refractory stone, and allow it to cook for about 5-7 minutes.

Before serving add some flakes of pecorino cheese.

Davide Civitiello HOMEMADE PIZZA

Ham and mushrooms

Recommended bases
→ p.29 Neapolitan
→ p.43 Whole wheat
→ p.43 Cereals
→ p.52 Gluten free

300 g button mushrooms
(or 150 g cream
of mushroom)
125 g Shredded buffalo
cheese
70 g cooked ham
Black pepper to taste
Basil to taste
1 garlic clove

EVO oil to taste
Oil for frying to taste

1 pizza

Sauté the mushrooms in a pan with EVO oil and a clove
of garlic , blend (after removing the garlic) until you reach
a creamy consistency. Allow to cool and set aside. Stretch out
the dough, spread the mushroom cream on the base
and sprinkle with a drizzle of EVO oil. Fry a few basil leaves
until crispy, drain and set aside.

For the baking process
Bake the pizza in a preheated oven at 230°C (or at maximum
power) on a refractory stone, and allow it to cook for about
5-7 minutes.

Once out of the oven, dress the pizza with shredded buffalo
cheese and cooked ham.
   Garnish with ground black pepper, fried basil leaves
and a drizzle of EVO oil.

Davide Civitiello HOMEMADE PIZZA

Nerano

Recommended bases
→ p.29 Neapolitan
→ p.43 Cereals
→ p.52 Gluten free

50 g Provolone
del Monaco cheese
30 g water
10 g EVO oil
100 g mozzarella
fiordilatte
100 g zucchini
5 slices of guanciale
(not too thin)
Mint leaves to taste
EVO oil to taste
Black pepper to taste

1 pizza

Grate the provolone cheese and blend it with water, 10 g EVO oil and a few mint leaves.

Cut the zucchini into thin slices, fry them in a little EVO oil until golden brown and keep the cooking oil on one side to use as a topping for pizza (it is aromatic and takes on a bright green color).

Brown the slices of guanciale in a preheated non-stick pan so that they become crunchy, then transfer it onto a paper towel so that the excess fat is absorbed.

Stretch out the dough and cover the base with the cream of provolone, then add the slices of zucchini and the diced fiordilatte.

For the baking process
Bake the pizza in a preheated oven at 230°C (or at maximum power) on a refractory stone, and allow it to cook for about 5-7 minutes.

Add the crispy guanciale once the pizza has been removed from the oven, a few mint leaves and a grind of black pepper.

Davide Civitiello HOMEMADE PIZZA

Oven fried pizza

Recommended bases
→ p.29 Neapolitan
→ p.52 Gluten free

50 g ricotta
1 Neapolitan tarallo
with lard and pepper
(→ p.132 Recipe)
50 g cracklings cut
into thin slices
Basil to taste
Black pepper to taste
Oil for frying to taste

1 pizza

Stretch out the pizza, fry it in plenty of hot oil in a preheated oven at 180°C until it inflates and golden on all sides.
Drain the fried pizza and transfer it onto a paper towel to pat dry the excess oil, then bake it for 3 minutes in a preheated oven at 230°C (or at maximum power) on a refractory stone.

Whilst the pizza is in the oven, in oil fry a few basil leaves until crispy, drain and set aside.

Spread the ricotta on the base of the pizza, add the cracklings, the coarsely crumbled tarallo and a grind of black pepper on top.

Garnish with the crunchy basil leaves.

Davide Civitiello HOMEMADE PIZZA

Calzone Scalorella

Recommended bases
→ p.29 Neapolitan

300 g escarole
20 g black olives
from Gaeta
5 g desalted capers
5 g pine nuts
1 fillet of anchovies
from Cetara
5 g raisins
100 g provola cheese
smoked
1 garlic clove
White wine to taste
EVO oil to taste

1 calzone

Blanch the escarole in salted boiling water, cut into small pieces and sauté in a pan with the garlic, EVO oil, the anchovy fillet, pitted olives, desalted capers, raisins (previously soaked in white wine) and pine nuts. Allow to cool and set on one side.

Stretch out the dough **(→ p.45 Masterclass)**, fill it with the sautéed escarole and the diced provola. Fold and seal, then decorate with the ingredients used for the filling.

For the baking process
Bake the calzone in a preheated oven at 230°C (or at maximum power) on a refractory stone, and allow it to cook for about 5-7 minutes.

Autumn garden ◉ Red lentils and guanciale ◉ Mortadella and lemon ◉ The Fan ◉ Yellow and green buffalo mozzarella ◉ Papaccelle peppers and spicy salami ◉ Pezzotto

Creative toppings

Creative toppings are some of signature pizzas developed during my career as a pizzaiolo. Ingredients and colors, but above all seasons and territories. Always start from the nature that surrounds you to create new delicious pizzas.

Davide Civitiello HOMEMADE PIZZA

Autumn garden

Recommended bases
→ p.29 Neapolitan
→ p.43 Whole wheat
→ p.43 Cereals
→ p.52 Gluten free

150 g yellow potatoes
60 g purple potatoes
60 g broccoli from Bari
150 g pumpkin
2 button mushrooms
50 g chickpeas flour
70 g water
Salt to taste
2 garlic cloves
EVO oil to taste

1 pizza

Dissolve the chickpeas flour in water, add a pinch of salt and mix it well.

Pour the mixture onto baking paper and bake at 150°C until all the water evaporates. Allow to cool and set aside the obtained wafer.

Boil the yellow and purple potatoes using two separate pots to prevent the colors from mixing.

Boil the broccoli and sauté the whole mushrooms in a pan with garlic and EVO oil.

In an iron skillet, sauté the pumpkin – previously cut into large pieces – with EVO oil, unpeeled garlic and a pinch of salt.

Once ready, remove the garlic and blend the pumpkin until it reaches a smooth and creamy texture.

Stretch out the pizza dough, then using a potato masher, press the yellow-fleshed potatoes straight onto the base. Add the broccoli, the coarsely mashed purple potatoes and the mushrooms cut roughly into slices (to prevent them from drying out during the cooking process).

Finish with quenelles of pumpkin cream.

For the baking process
Bake the pizza in a preheated oven at 230°C (or at maximum power) on a refractory stone, and allow it to cook for about 5-7 minutes.

Garnish with pieces of the chickpea wafer.

Davide Civitiello HOMEMADE PIZZA

Red lentils and guanciale

Recommended bases
→ p.29 Neapolitan
→ p.43 Whole wheat
→ p.52 Gluten free

30 g red lentil flour
120 g water
120 g mozzarella fiordilatte
80 g red datterini cherry tomatoes
35 g guanciale
EVO oil to taste
Parsley to taste
Salt to taste

1 pizza

Dissolve the lentils flour in the water with a pinch of salt and allow the cream to thicken at 60°C.

Cover the base of the pizza with the cream, add the diced fiordilatte cheese, the datterini cherry tomatoes cut in half and the guanciale cut into thin slices.

For the baking process
Bake the pizza in a preheated oven at 230°C (or at maximum power) on a refractory stone, and allow it to cook for about 5-7 minutes.

Remove from the oven and sprinkle the pizza with chopped parsley.

Davide Civitiello HOMEMADE PIZZA

Mortadella and lemon

Recommended bases
→ p.29 Neapolitan
→ p.43 Cereals
→ p.53 Gluten free

120 g mozzarella fiordilatte
20 g untreated lemon from Sorrento
80 g PGI Bologna Mortadella
20 g pistachios from Bronte
Black pepper to taste

1 pizza

Wash the lemon well and cut it into thin slices, incise each slice so as to cut it in half and use the slices as if they were 'fillets'. Stretch out the dough and place the lemon fillets on the base, then add the diced fiordilatte.

For the baking process
Bake the pizza in a preheated oven at 230°C (or at maximum power) on a refractory stone, and allow it to cook for about 5-7 minutes.

Remove from the oven and complete with thin slices of mortadella, lightly toasted pistachios and a sprinkling of black pepper.

Davide Civitiello HOMEMADE PIZZA

The Fan

Recommended bases
→ p.29 Neapolitan
→ p.43 Cereals

65 g Parma dry-cured ham
250 g PDO buffalo
mozzarella from
Campania
Rocket salad to taste
Basil mayonnaise to taste
EVO oil to taste

1 pizza

Stretch out the pizza, grease the base using the EVO oil
so that the two halves do not stick together during
the cooking process, then fold the base in half.

For the baking process
Bake the pizza in a preheated oven at 230°C (or at maximum
power) on a refractory stone, and allow it to cook for about
5-7 minutes.

Unfold the pizza and stuff it with rocket salad, then
the sliced Buffalo Mozzarella, sliced dry cured ham
and a basil mayonnaise.

Davide Civitiello HOMEMADE PIZZA

Yellow and green buffalo mozzarella

Recommended bases
→ p.29 Neapolitan
→ p.43 Whole wheat
→ p.43 Cereals
→ p.52 Gluten free

130 g yellow datterini
cherry tomatoes
150 g PDO buffalo
mozzarella from
Campania
Basil to taste
EVO oil to taste
Salt to taste

1 pizza

Make a light sauce by blending the basil along with EVO oil and salt.

Stretch out the dough and, on the base, add the yellow datterini cherry tomatoes, partially lightly pressed, and partially cut in half.

Then add the sliced Buffalo Mozzarella, previously cut so that it loses the excess water.

For the baking process
Bake the pizza in a preheated oven at 230°C (or at maximum power) on a refractory stone, and allow it to cook for about 5-7 minutes.

Remove from the oven and dress with the sauce.

Papaccelle peppers and spicy salami

Recommended bases
→ **p.29 Neapolitan**
→ **p.43 Cereals**
→ **p.52 Gluten free**

100 g yellow and red
papaccelle peppers
(small sweet peppers)
120 g mozzarella
fiordilatte
30 g spicy salami
1 garlic clove
Parsley to taste
EVO oil to taste

1 pizza

Cut the papaccelle and sauté them in a pan with EVO oil and unpeeled garlic.

Stretch out the pizza and sprinkle the diced fiordilatte on the base.

Then add the papaccelle.

For the baking process
Bake the pizza in a preheated oven at 230°C (or at maximum power) on a refractory stone, and allow it to cook for about 5-7 minutes.

Complete with thinly sliced spicy salami and finely chopped parsley.

Pezzotto

Recommended bases
→ p.29 Neapolitan

100 g buffalo ricotta
100 g eggplant parmigiana
50 g provola
Basil to taste
EVO oil to taste

1 pizza

Stretch out the pizza following the same method used to roll out a calzone, spread the ricotta along the entire border and fold the edges to create a stuffed cornicione.

Cut the parmigiana into cubes and place them on the base. Finally, add the provola cut into strips.

For the baking process
Bake the pizza in a preheated oven at 230°C (or at maximum power) on a refractory stone, and allow it to cook for about 5-7 minutes.

Remove from the oven and garnish with a few basil leaves and a drizzle of EVO oil.

Zeppole di San Giuseppe ○ Struffoli ○ Wheat Pastiera ○ Roccocò ○ Graffa ○ Traditional Casatiello ○ Whole wheat Casatiello ○ Gluten free Tortano ○ Taralli with lard and pepper ○ Deep-dish with eggplant parmigiana ○ Neapolitan panini ○ Savory Danubio ○ Sweet Danubio ○ Sour cherry biscuits ○ Baba

Holiday recipes

In Naples, cuisine is made up of history, imagination, work and passion of all those who, every day, give life to the products and dishes of one of the richest gastronomic traditions in Italy. However, in Naples, cooking is also something else, it's a party!

During the holidays, the city and its kitchens explode with colors and scents, and people do nothing but celebrate the pleasure of eating well with their beloved ones.

Christmas, Easter, the all Saints days – the recipes of the holiday season are many and varied, and now I would like to tell you my favorites,the various steps and tricks to prepare them in the best way. In order to do this, I summoned a great friend of mine and a professional, Antonio Sorrentino, a cook of the Neapolitan tradition, generous and competent, a companion of thousands of adventures. All the recipes share the presence of the dough: sweet and savory, simple or complex, together with Antonio we will explain how to make such Neapolitan holiday-season dishes to transmit great emotions.

For a start, zeppole di San Giuseppe, with custard and black cherries: despite being designed for Father's Day they can be eaten all year round, delicious and soft as they are. Whilst, at Christmas, the first culinary firework explode: struffoli, for example, so colorful, with an intense honey flavor, and roccocò, biscuits made in the occasion of the Immaculate Conception that accompany the whole holiday season until the Epiphany, with their mix of spices and citrus. Carnival time is the triumph of fried foods, with graffa, a sugary and soft cake – almost like a doughnut – that is among the most consumed on the streets of the city. With the Easter calendar comes the queen, the famous wheat pastiera, the authentic one that the whole world envies us, scented with orange flowers. But also casatiello , in a double version – traditional and whole wheat – a bread enriched with eggs, meats and cheeses, or tortano, a rustic Neapolitan cake, also in a gluten free version, soft, with whole eggs. Among other delights I also mentioned the appetizing Neapolitan rolls, using a quick dough enriched with mortadella, cracklings and mixed cheeses, or the famous Danubio, in its sweet and savory versions, absolutely not to be cut with a knife but 'pinched' with your fingers. Then, taralli with almonds and pepper can't be missed, to accompany Sunday lunches or anniversaries. For those who are not yet satisfied with such holiday recipes, please help yourself to sour cherry biscuits, so rich with ingredients such as Strega liqueur, cocoa, chopped hazelnuts and orange peel, that can be made either with sponge cake or leftover brioche, panettone and any stale sweet dough. And – equally unforgettable – the Neapolitan babà, a risen dessert whose procedure might be, perhaps, a bit cumbersome to perform, but certainly worth it: light, spongy and aromatic, with a characteristic taste of citrus and rum.

And finally, a glorious homage to the USA, the deep dish. Originally it is the name of a typical American pizza, from Chicago to be precise, and together with Antonio Sorrentino we chose to reinterpret it as a Neapolitan 'stuffed pizza', yes, stuffed with a dish that reflects Naples in all its taste: the eggplant parmigiana.

As you can see, the red thread of the baking art and dough runs through all holidays, and it is the basis for sweet and savory recipes, designed to uplift many moments of celebration, with friends and family, not only at the table but also in the kitchen, getting your hand dirty with flour.

Davide and chef Antonio Sorrentino in Naples

Antonio Sorrentino

He was born in Torre del Greco on August 3rd, 1967, inheriting the passion for cooking from his father Aniello, a life mentor and professional coach. He grows up cultivating a love for the land and cooking by observing his grandmothers who, every day, in their 'gastronomic shops' of the time, prepared dishes promptly dictated by seasonality and tradition. Antonio is a small-big chef-artist, who skillfully juggles by playing with the products of his beloved Campania region.

His cuisine is never banal, always surprising and characterized by the use of excellent raw materials, harmoniously combining the past (the recipes of his grandmothers, his aunt Teresa and her great dad) and the present, made up of contaminations and creative trends.

He carried out all kinds of duties in the restaurant industry, working his way up from an early age in many hotels and restaurants, both in Campania and Italy. He was also a professional rugby player and since 1994 he has been in charge as executive chef of the SEBETO SPA group, owner of important brands in the catering industry such as Rossopomodoro, Ham Holy Burger, Rossosapore and Anema e Cozze, with more than 150 restaurants in the whole world.

For all of them, he deals with market analysis, business plans, management and design of spaces, as well as the dynamics of restaurant formats, the definition of the gastronomic offer, food cost (choice of products and suppliers) and the selection and training of staff. Since '99 he has been a food and wine teacher in hotel establishments between Capri, Ischia, Ercolano and Naples, whilst since 2012 he is also a freelance journalist and author of books on cooking and the world of pizza, as well as the protagonist of various television programs and one of the most beloved chefs in the Youtube channel of ItaliaSquisita.

He is also a UNICEF testimonial in Campania.

Zeppole di San Giuseppe

Difficulty ●●●　　🕐 1h 30min　　✳ Father's Day

For the custard
50 g rice starch
250 g milk
Zest of ½ untreated lemon
from Sorrento
100 g sugar
4 yolks
½ vanilla pod

For the dough
250 ml water
10 g salt
100 g butter
230 g 00 strong flour
6 eggs
Oil for frying as needed

For the garnish
Sour cherries in syrup
to taste
Powdered sugar to taste

8 zeppole

For the custard
Beat the egg yolks with sugar in a bowl until the mixture is light and creamy. Add the sifted rice starch and the milk, previously heated with the lemon peel and vanilla.
Mix and combine well using a whisk, until the cream is soft and without lumps. Cook the cream in a saucepan over a low heat, stirring constantly. Bring to a boil and cook for 2 more minutes. When it thickens, remove from the heat and allow it to cool.

For the dough
Pour the water into a thick-bottomed saucepan, add the salt, the diced butter and bring to a boil. When the butter has melted and the water comes to a boil, remove the saucepan from the heat, add the flour to the mixture and mix well with a wooden ladle until the dough becomes compact.
Return the saucepan to a low heat and stir the mixture until a whitish glaze forms on the bottom. Turn off the heat, then transfer the dough into a bowl and allow it to cool. Add the eggs to the mixture, one at a time, only after each of them has been completely absorbed. Allow the dough to rest in the refrigerator for 30 minutes.

Then cut out squares of baking paper.

Pour the mixture into a pastry bag with a star-shaped spout and, with a spiral movement, form a disc of dough of 10 cm in diameter onto each square. Still proceeding with a circular motion, create another disc of dough on top. Zeppole must develop in height.

In the meantime, heat abundant oil for frying in two pans: in the first one, the oil must be at a temperature of about 130°C and the second, with oil at 180°C.

Dip the zeppole in the first pan (no more than 2-3 at a time) still attached to the squares of baking paper. The paper will come off by itself after a few seconds. You remove it with kitchen tongs. When the zeppole puff, transfer them into the other pan and cook by turning them often until golden brown.

Once ready, drain the excess oil by placing them on absorbent kitchen paper.

For the garnish

When the zeppole are cooled down, pour the custard into a pastry bag with a star-shaped spout and stuff them in the center with the cream.

Garnish with 2-3 sour cherries in syrup on top and a dusting of icing sugar before serving.

→ Zeppole can also be baked in the oven: arrange them well spaced on a baking tray lined with baking paper and bake them at 190°C for about 25 minutes without opening the oven

→ This is the traditional recipe from Campania, but every Italian region has its own typical and different version

→ A single-portion dessert, it can also be made in a 'cake' version: the zeppolone

Struffoli

Difficulty ●○○   ⏱ 4h   ✳ Christmas

For the dough
500 g 00 weak flour
3 eggs
50 g sugar
60 g leaf lard (or butter)
150 g anisette (or dry
Marsala, or Vermouth)
Grated zest of 1 untreated
lemon from Sorrento
Grated zest of 1 orange
1 sachet of vanilla
1 pinch of salt
Oil for frying as needed

For the dressing
500 g honey
80 g sugar
25 g diavulilli (mixed
colored or silvered
sprinkles)
100 g candied orange peel
100 g candied citron
50 g candied cherries

**2 trays of 24 cm
in diameter**

For the dough
Combine all the ingredients well together and allow to rest
for two hours in a bowl covered with a kitchen cloth.
    Then form cylinders of dough and cut out small pieces
of the size of a hazelnut. Keep the struffoli on a tray and well
dusted with flour before cooking to prevent them
from sticking together.
    Sift the struffoli in order to remove the excess flour and
dip-fry them in hot oil in several batches, paying attention
to maintain the oil temperature constant at 170°C.
    Once golden but not too brownish, drain and transfer them
onto a plate covered with absorbent paper.

For the dressing
Melt the honey and sugar over a low heat in a fairly large pot
and pour the struffoli into it, stirring until well coated with
honey. Then pour about 1/3 of the sugared almonds and
the candied fruit cut into small pieces, and mix gently.
    Arrange the struffoli on the serving dish and garnish with
the rest of the sprinkles and candied fruit.
    Allow to cool and serve.

Davide Civitiello HOMEMADE PIZZA

Wheat pastiera

Difficulty ●●○   ⊕ 3h   ＊ Easter

For the shortcrust pastry
500 g 00 weak flour
200 g cow's milk butter
200 g sugar
1 whole egg
2 egg yolks
½ sachet of vanilla
flavoring
Grated untreated lemon
from Sorrento zest to taste
Grated orange zest to
taste

For the filling
500 g buffalo or cow's
milk ricotta
450 g sugar
290 g cooked wheat (also
in cans)
1 untreated lemon from
Sorrento
15 g candied citron
15 g candied orange peel
Cinnamon powder to taste
100 g milk
25 gr of butter
4 eggs + 1 yolk
½ sachet of vanilla
flavoring (or ½ pure vanilla
pod)
1 phial of wildflower water

1 tray
24 cm wide × 6 cm high

For the shortcrust pastry
Spread the flour onto the working surface in a fountain shape
and put the cold butter into small pieces in the center together
with the vanilla flavoring, the citrus peel, sugar and mix
everything rapidly with your fingertips, as if you are snapping
them, forming a crumble. Break the eggs into a container,
beat them and incorporate them into the crumbled dough
until a soft and smooth dough is obtained. Shape into a ball,
cover with cling film and leave to rest in the refrigerator
for 30 minutes.

For the filling
A few hours before making the pastiera, drain the ricotta
using a sieve. Meanwhile, pour the cooked wheat into
a saucepan, add milk, butter, lemon zest and slowly cook
for 30 minutes, stirring often so as to make the mixture
creamy. Then, allow it to cool and set on one side.
    In a bowl put the 4 whole eggs, the yolk and mix with sugar,
then gradually add the ricotta, stirring with a whisk.
Add the vanilla flavoring, a pinch of ground cinnamon and
the wildflower water to the mixture. Work everything until
the mixture becomes smooth. Then add the grated lemon peel
and the diced candied fruit. Mix everything with the cooked
cream of wheat.

To finish the pastiera
Roll out the shortcrust pastry using a rolling pin, creating
a disc, ½ cm thick, then line the greased tray. Cut out the

excess dough, roll it out again and cut it into strips.
Pour the previously prepared creamy mixture to level the
pastiera. Garnish the surface of the pastiera with the strips
of dough arranged so as to create a diamond-shaped net.
Finally, brush with a beaten egg and bake at 165°C for
45 minutes, until the pastiera takes on a light amber color.
Remove from the oven and let it cool.

→ The shortcrust pastry should be worked
quickly to avoid overheating the butter
and obtaining a dough that is too soft

→ Pastiera was born as a typical Easter dessert
but now, in Naples, it is eaten all year round

Davide Civitiello HOMEMADE PIZZA

Roccocò

Difficulty ●○○　　🕐 1h 30min　　✳ Christmas

1 kg 00 medium
strength flour
900 g sugar
900 g unpeeled almonds
Grated peel of 1 large
orange
Peel of 3 mandarins
Grated peel of 1 untreated
lemon from Sorrento
25 g pisto (mix of spices:
cinnamon, cloves,
nutmeg, cardamom)
2 g ammonia for cakes
(or powdered ammonium
bicarbonate)
150 g candied fruit (orange
and citron)
100 ml warm water
50 g honey
300 ml orange and
tangerine juice
1 sachet of vanilla flavoring
Salt to taste
Water as needed

To decorate
2 eggs
1 teaspoon of sugar
100 g almonds

30 pieces of 100 g each

Lightly toast the almonds, allow them to cool, then coarsely chop them leaving some whole for decoration.

Place the flour onto a counter in a fountain shape, then add the sugar, the chopped almonds, the grated lemon and orange peel, the diced mandarin peel, the pisto, the cubed candied fruit and the vanilla flavoring.

Separately, squeeze the citrus fruits, filter the juice, add water and allow it to warm over a low heat. Remove from the heat. So, melt the honey, add the ammonia and gradually pour over the dough.

Work all the ingredients by hand, gradually adding the lukewarm liquid. Combine the mixture well so as to obtain a soft but not sticky dough.

Then, cut the dough into pieces of 100 g each, forming cylinders with your hands and shape the donuts.

Line a large baking tray with baking paper and transfer the roccocos on top.

It is important to leave them far enough apart from each other to prevent them from sticking together during cooking.

To decorate
Place 4 almonds on each roccocò, pressing them lightly so as they adhere to the dough.

Brush the surface with the eggs beaten with sugar and bake at 150°C for about 30/40 minutes.

Remove the roccocos from the oven, turn them over and allow them to cool.

Graffa

Difficulty ●●○   ⊕ 2h   ✳ Carnival

500 g 00 strong flour
10 g active dry yeast
(or 20 g of fresh
brewer's yeast)
15 g sugar
10 g salt
Strega liqueur to taste
Vanilla essence to taste
100 g egg (about 2egg)
250 g milk
60 g butter
Grated peel of ½
untreated lemon from
Sorrento
Grated peel of ½ orange
Fine granulated sugar
to taste
Oil for frying to taste

**12 graffe of about
80 g each**

Add the flour and baking powder in a stand mixer with
a dough hook. Separately, mix the eggs with the milk and
start adding the liquid in the mixer. Then add salt, sugar,
vanilla, the Strega liqueur and the grated peel of lemon and
orange. Finally, stir in the cold butter cut into small pieces.

Allow it to rise first as a single mass until doubled
(about 1 hour and a half), then shape the graffe: cut the dough
into pieces of about 80 g each, create cylinders 20 cm long
and seal by crossing them in a bow. Transfer the graffe onto
a floured tray, well spaced, and allow them to rise in a warm
place until they double in size (about 1 hour).

Dip-fry in hot oil at 180°C, pat-dry using absorbent paper
and toss with fine granulated sugar whilst still hot.

Davide Civitiello HOMEMADE PIZZA

Traditional Casatiello

Difficulty ●●○   🕐 6h   ✳ Easter

For the dough
1 kg 00 strong flour
700 g water
25 g salt
10 g active dry yeast
(or 20 g of fresh
brewer's yeast)
100 g leaf lard (or lard)

For the filling
300 g Napoli type salami
300 g Neapolitan
cracklings
300 g fresh provolone
100 g grated pecorino
romano
6 eggs
200 g leaf lard (or lard)
Black pepper to taste
Salt to taste

**1 tray with a hole
of 30 cm in diameter**

Pour ¾ of the flour into one half of a large bowl, pour all the water and dissolve the salt into the other half.

Then add the yeast into the flour and start kneading the flour with your fingers, mixing well so as to avoid lumps. Then add the rest of the flour and the leaf lard, continuing to knead until the leaf lard is completely absorbed. Transfer the dough onto a counter and kneading vigorously for about 10 minutes until the dough becomes smooth and compact. Make a loaf, put it back in the bowl and let it rest for 60 minutes, covered with cling film.

Cut into cubes all the meats and cheeses and, separately, beat 2 whole eggs with a pinch of salt, ground black pepper and 50 g of grated pecorino.

Take the risen dough and, on a counter, dusted with flours stretch it out with a rolling pin (setting aside a piece of dough of about 100 g).

Spread out the dough and sprinkle the surface with the diced mixture, the beaten egg, the remaining pecorino cheese and a generous handful of black pepper.

Distribute the leaf lard over the entire surface and roll the dough onto itself.

Seal the two ends by lining them so as to form a donut in order to prevent the filling from leaking out during the baking process. Grease the baking mould with leaf lard and transfer the casatiello into it.

Take the 4 remaining eggs, wash them well, dry them and place them on the surface of the casatiello until they sink halfway.

Using the 100 g of the remaining dough, form strips and arrange them criss crossed over the eggs.

Spread the whole casatiello with the remaining leaf lard and allow it to rise once again until it triples in volume (about 2 hours). Bake in a preheated oven at 165°C for about 1 hour and a half.

Whole wheat Casatiello

Difficulty ●●○   ⏲ 6h   ✳ Easter

For the dough
500 g whole wheat flour
500 g 00 strong flour
700 g water
25 g salt
10 g active dry yeast
(or 20 g of fresh
brewer's yeast)
100 g leaf lard

**1 tray with a hole
of 30 cm in diameter**

To make a whole wheat casatiello, the white flour is added first and, only after, the whole wheat one.

The procedure and the ingredients on the same as the traditional casatiello.

→ Casatiello seems to take its name from 'caso' which in Neapolitan means cheese, a plausible hypothesis given the abundance of cheese inside. Tortano, on the other hand, contains a denial of its identity in its name: torta-no, it's not a cake

Gluten free Tortano

Difficulty ●●○ ⏲ 3h ✳ Easter

For the dough
1 kg gluten free flour
10 g active dry yeast
(or 20 g of fresh
brewer's yeast)
800 g water
25 g fine salt
100 g leaf lard (or EVO oil
or lard)

For the filling
300 g Napoli type salami
300 g Neapolitan
cracklings
300 g fresh provolone
100 g grated pecorino
romano
4 hard boiled eggs
50 g leaf lard (or lard)
Black pepper to taste

**1 tray with a hole
of 30 cm in diameter**

Mix the flour, the yeast and water for about 3 minutes using a stand mixer with a flat beater. Then, add the salt and let it work for another minute. Finally, add the leaf lard. Cut all the meats and cheeses into cubes and incorporate them into the dough. Place the dough in a donut cake-mould, well greased with leaf lard. Add the hard boiled eggs, with the shell, into the dough and allow it to rise until it triples in volume (about 2 hours). Spread the tortano with leaf lard and bake in a preheated oven at 165°C for about 50-60 minutes.

Taralli with lard and pepper

Difficulty ●●○   ⏲ 1h 40min   ✳ Holidays

100 g 00 strong flour
400 g 00 weak flour
250 g unpeeled almonds
180 g water
7,5 g active dry yeast
(or 15 g of fresh
brewer's yeast)
250 g leaf lard (or lard)
20 g salt
10 g black pepper
5 g honey

24 taralli of 50 g each

In a big bowl make the 'starting yeast' by combining 60 g water, honey, 100 g of strong flour and all the yeast. Knead roughly, cover the bowl and allow it to rest in a warm place (in a turned off oven with the light on) until its volume has doubled (approximately 1 hour). In the meantime, toast 200 g almonds on a tray lined with baking paper at 200°C for 8 minutes. Once cooled, crush them roughly with the help of a rolling pin.

Once the starting yeast is ready, knead it along with the remaining flour, then add the leaf lard and only at the end, the salt and black pepper.

Move the dough onto a counter and knead it for an additional 10 minutes until you obtain a smooth and soft dough. At this point, add the crushed almonds and combine them well with the dough.

Allow the final dough to rest for a few minutes and start the cutting phase. Obtain pieces of 25 g each (48 pieces in order to obtain 24 taralli) and create sausages that are 25 cm long from each piece. Join the sausages two by two, braid them as a rope and seal the edges so as to obtain a doughnut shaped tarallo. Garnish the taralli by distributing the almonds (lightly wet to prevent them from detaching from the dough during the baking process) on the surface. Allow them to rise until they double in volume (approximately 1 hour and a half).

Bake in a preheated oven at 170°C for about 50/60 minutes. The taralli will be ready when they get golden brown.

Davide Civitiello HOMEMADE PIZZA

Deep-dish with eggplant parmigiana

Difficulty ●●●   🕓 4h   ✳ Sunday

For the dough

1 kg 00 strong flour
600 g water
25 g salt
10 g active dry yeast
(or 20 g of fresh
brewer's yeast)
100 g leaf lard (or lard)
8 g sugar

For the garnish

2 kg long eggplants
1,5 kg pureed San
Marzano tomatoes
600 g smoked scamorza
300 g grated grana
cheese
1 onion
Grated grana to taste
Basil to taste
Flour to taste
100 g EVO oil to taste
Oil for frying to taste
Butter to taste
Salt to taste
Black pepper to taste
Water to taste

**1 tray with a lock
of 30 cm in diameter**

Wash the eggplants and cut lengthwise into slices about ½ cm thick.

Arrange them in a colander, sprinkling with salt each layer and allow them to drain for about 1 hour with a weight on top.

Then, remove the excess salt and water, pat dry the eggplant slices, lightly dust them with flour and dip-fry in abundant oil at 180°C.

Once golden brown, drain them with the help of a skimmer and pat-dry the excess oil with kitchen paper.

In the meantime, sauté the chopped onion in a large pan with 100 g of EVO oil. Add the tomato puree and a glass of water, season with a few basil leaves cut coarsely with your hands, then adjust with salt. Allow the sauce to cook for 30 minutes, stirring occasionally. Then, allow it to cool.

In a bowl, dissolve the yeast, the leaf lard and sugar by gradually adding water.

Add half the flour, mix, then add the salt, kneading the dough very vigorously for a few minutes.

Gradually add the rest of the flour and continue to knead the mixture until it comes off the sides of the bowl.

Transfer the dough onto a counter and knead it vigorously for about 20 minutes.

Shape a loaf, cover with a cloth and let it rest for 1 hour.

Divide the dough into blocks, roll out the dough using a rolling pin. Line the bottom of the tray and the edges with the dough.

Pour a veil of tomato sauce at the bottom and start arranging the first layer of fried eggplants on it by slightly overlapping each slice.

Sprinkle with the grated grana cheese, a few hand-shredded basil leaves and tomato sauce.

Then cover with smoked scamorza cut into quite thin slices and continue to stratify in this order up to the edge of the tray.

Roll out the remaining dough and make a disc as large as the size of the tray. Place it on top, so as to cover the layers of eggplant, seal the edges well and remove the excess dough. Cover with tomato sauce, grated grana and a drizzle of melted butter.

Bake in a preheated oven in static mode at 180°C for about 30 minutes. Remove from the oven and allow it to rest for a few minutes before cutting.

→ The deep-dish is a pizza of American origin. I reinterpreted it by taking inspiration from the Neapolitan pizza piena (stuffed pizza). I chose to stuff it with eggplant parmigiana, a symbolic dish of Neapolitan cuisine

Neapolitan panini

Difficulty ●●○   ⏱ 6h   ✳ Holidays

For the dough
500 g 00 strong flour
300 g water
50 g leaf lard (or lard)
15 g table salt
3 g active dry yeast
(or 6 g of fresh
brewer's yeast)

For the filling
100 g Napoli salami
100 g fresh provolone
cheese
100 g Neapolitan pork
cracklings (or mortadella
or baked ham)
Grated pecorino romano
to taste
3 hard boiled eggs
Salt to taste
Black pepper to taste
1 yolk
Milk to taste

**8 big or 16 small
sandwiches**

Pour ¾ of the flour into one half of a big bowl and pour all the water and salt into the other half. Add the yeast into the flour and start kneading, trying to avoid lumps. Gradually add the flour until it becomes a dough and, finally, add the leaf lard.

Transfer the mixture onto a working surface and continue kneading energetically for about 10 minutes until you obtain a smooth and compact dough. Shape it into a ball, cover the bowl and allow the dough to rest for 60 minutes. Cook the three eggs and, in the meantime, cut the cured meats and the cheeses into cubes. Then, stretch out the dough onto a counter that is lightly dusted with flour, forming a 40×30 cm rectangle, 1cm thick.

Cover the surface with the mix of cured meats and cheeses cut into cubes, a dust of black pepper and the hard-boiled eggs cut into pieces. Lightly press the dough with your hands so that the pieces gently sink into the dough and sprinkle with grated pecorino cheese.

Gently roll the rectangle up from the long side, and form a roll. Then cut it into regular pieces of about 5 cm.

Move the rolls onto a tray lined with baking paper, and allow to rise, covered with a cloth, for about one hour and a half. Once risen, brush the dough with a yolk whisked together with 2 teaspoons of milk.

Bake in a preheated oven at 180°C in a static mode for approximately 25 minutes. Remove from the oven and allow to cool, covered with a cotton cloth.

Davide Civitiello HOMEMADE PIZZA

Savory Danubio

Difficulty ●●○　　🕐 4h　　✳ Sunday

For the dough
500 g 00 strong flour
15 g active dry yeast
(or 30 g of fresh
brewer's yeast)
125 g water
125 g eggs
40 g sugar
20 g salt
75 g butter

For the filling
1 egg
100 g cooked ham
100 g gruyere type cheese

**1 tray with a lock
with a 30 cm diameter**

For the dough
Add the flour into the bowl of a stand mixer, with a dough hook, then add the yeast.

In a separate bowl, beat the eggs and water with a fork.

In the stand mixer, start incorporating part of the liquids to the solid ingredients and, after a few minutes, add salt, sugar and add the remaining liquid. Finally, add the butter cut into chunks.

Work the dough in the machine for about 15 minutes and, then, finish the dough by kneading it by hand. Allow the dough to rest for 40 minutes in a bowl, covered on top (until the volume is doubled). Then, cut the dough into pieces of the same size and create balls.

For the filling
Gently stretch out the dough, add the previously diced cheese and cooked ham (prosciutto cotto) in the middle and combine the flaps by forming precise and consistent balls.
Then arrange them following a radial pattern (with their closure below) along the entire diameter of a previously greased round baking tray.

Finally, brush the surface with a beaten egg to prevent the dough from drying during rising and allow it to rise until doubled in volume (for about 1 hour). Bake in the oven at 180°C for about 30 minutes.

Sweet Danubio

Difficulty ●●○   ⊕ 6h   ✳ Sunday

For the dough
500 g 00 strong flour
15 g active dry yeast
(or 30 g of fresh
brewer's yeast)
125 g water
125 g eggs
50 g sugar
10 g salt
100 g butter
Vanilla to taste
Grated peel of an
untreated lemon
from Sorrento
Grated peel of an orange

Fot the garnish
1 egg
Granulated sugar to taste
Icing sugar to taste

**1 tray with a lock
with a 30 cm diameter**

◍ For this sweet version with no filling, the procedure and the ingredients of the dough are the same of the savory version, but in slightly different proportions

Once the surface of the balls is brushed with the beaten egg, add the granulated sugar before baking so as to give a rustic and crunchy effect. Allow it to rise until doubled in volume (about 1 hour) and bake in the oven at 170°C for about 30 minutes.
    Sprinkle it with icing sugar before serving.

→ Work the dough starting from the solid ingredients as it needs to develop a lot of strength

→ The butter is used to give shininess and make the dough softer

→ The egg brushed on the surface helps keep the dough moist during the rising but it also gives the danubio a nice golden color during baking

→ The sweet Danubio can be filled with hazelnut cream or custard. The balls can be filled before or after baking

Davide Civitiello HOMEMADE PIZZA

Sour cherry biscuits

Difficulty ●●○   🕐 1h + preparation time for the shortcrust pastry   ✳ Holidays

500 g 00 weak flour
250 g butter
250 g sugar
2 eggs
3 g salt
Vanilla pods to taste
Orange peel to taste
300 g sour cherries
compote
250 g stale sponge cake
(or any leftover brioche
or cake, even panettone)
60 g bitter cocoa
7 g Strega liquor to taste
Chopped hazelnuts
to taste
1 egg for brushing
1 teaspoon of sugar

8 biscuits

First make the shortcrust pastry: shape the flour into a fountain onto a working surface and, in the center, add the cold butter cut into cubes, vanilla, the grated peel of an orange and the sugar. Knead all the ingredients very roughly so as to obtain crumbles, the so-called 'sbriciolata'.

In a bowl break the eggs and beat them, then combine them with the sbriciolata until you obtain a soft and smooth dough. Shape the dough into a ball, seal it with cling film and allow it to rest in the refrigerator for 30 minutes.

In the meantime, in a kneading machine set with a flat beater add the broken sponge cake, the sour cherry compote, the cocoa and the Strega liquor. Mix until all the ingredients are well combined. Move the mixture onto a sheet of baking paper set onto a working surface and, with the help of a scraper, create a rectangle 38×10 cm, of a thickness of 4 cm. Store in the refrigerator for 30 minutes.

Remove the shortcrust pastry from the refrigerator and stretch it onto a surface dusted with flour, creating a rectangle that is 40 cm long and 28 cm wide with a thickness of about half cm. In the middle of the rectangle place the sour cherry mixture, remove the baking paper and use a scraper to level off the border of the shortcrust pastry so that the two edges line up and cover the filling without overlapping. Cut the excess dough away and fold the two edges towards the center by gently pinching them with your fingertips so that they adhere perfectly. Then turn upside down onto a tray lined with baking paper and store into the refrigerator for at least 10 minutes.

Once again, remove the loaf of sour cherries shortcrust pastry from the refrigerator and cover the surface with an egg beaten with sugar, then dust it with crumbled hazelnuts.

Cut out 8 biscuits, 5 cm wide and place them onto a baking tray lined with baking paper. Bake in a preheated static oven at 175°C in the middle level for 20-25 minutes. Remove the sour cherry biscuits from the oven and allow them to cool.

Davide Civitiello HOMEMADE PIZZA

Baba

Difficulty ●●●　　🕐 1h + rising and cooking time　　✳ Sunday

For the dough
250 g 00 strong flour
6 eggs
75 g cold butter
25 g sugar
4 g active dry yeast
(or 8 g of fresh
brewer's yeast)
6 g salt
5 g honey
60 g water

For the syrup
500 g water
200g sugar
80 ml rum
Untreated lemon from
Sorrento peel to taste
Orange peel to taste

For the glazing
Apricot jam to taste
Water to taste

10-12 babas

For the dough
In a bowl create the 'starting yeast' by combining 60 g water,
honey, 100 g flour weighed from the total amount and all
of the yeast.

Knead rapidly, cover the bowl and leave in a warm place
(in a turned off oven with the light on) until the volume
doubles (approximately 1 hour).

Add the flour and the sugar into a kneading machine with
a hook and start working the dough by adding, one at a time,
the first 3 eggs. When the dough reaches a good texture,
add salt and continue kneading while adding the other eggs
(remember to keep one aside that will be added at the end),
always allowing the previous one to absorb well.

Then add the butter in flakes and, finally, the last egg.
The mixture must be elastic, smooth and solid. If the baba
is well kneaded, we should obtain a veil effect by stretching
out a piece of dough.

Cover the dough and allow it to rise for approximately
30-40 minutes (it should double its volume).

Grease with butter 12 single-portion moulds or a classic
bigger mould (28 cm diameter baba savarin, with an
undulating edge, ring-shaped, like a doughnut). Once the
rising time has ended, start kneading the dough again and,
with a hand greased with butter, turn the dough around your
hands (in the jargon of pastry chefs this operation is called
'last beating').

Then add the dough into the single moulds by keeping
it 1,5 cm below the edge (60 g of dough in each mould, all
of the dough if using the big mould), place the moulds onto
a baking tray and allow to rise until the dough overflows
the edge, creating a nice little dome on its surface
(approximately 2 hours).

Bake the baba in a preheated oven at 180°C for about
20 minutes if using the single-portion moulds, or 30 minutes
if using the single mould (you can make sure that it baked all
the way through with the 'toothpick' method: insert a wooden
toothpick halfway through the mould – if the stick remains
dry and clean, the babas are ready). The babas must have
a golden brownish color. Once ready, remove from the oven
and allow to cool before removing them from the moulds.
The babas must cool down at 18-22°C and must be kept aside,
well covered and sealed until the next day: it is advisable
to dip the babas in rum when well stabilized only.

For the syrup
Add all the ingredients in a pot, except the rum, then bring
the syrup to a boil: once warm, add the rum. Use the syrup
at a temperature of about 45-50°C. Place the cooled babas onto
a grill set on a baking tray and start bathing them using a ladle
so that the syrup is well absorbed. The operation must be
repeated several times, saving all the liquid dripped on the tray
and, should it be necessary, bringing it back to a temperature
of 45-50°C. The babas should become soft and puffy, just like
a sponge.

For the glazing
Allow to cool for a few minutes and brush the surface with
apricot jam diluted with a little water. Store in the refrigerator.

→ The first rule for a baba is to never be in a hurry! The ingredients must be kneaded gently and slowly. They should be well incorporated, otherwise you may ruin the dough

→ Babas can be enriched by serving them with custard and sour cherries, or with fresh whipped cream and wild strawberries

→ Originating from Poland, babas move to the court of the King of France and finally reach Naples with the Monzu cooks, becoming one of the most iconic desserts of Naples and Italy

Flours

Yeasts

Ovens

Now it's time for us to take a few steps back and examine the matter in depth. It's time to talk about the three main elements every pizza is made of: flour, yeast and heat.

With the help of several technicians and specialists we will analyze them thoroughly, to try and resolve any doubt and thus acquire a more specific knowledge.

So, what are the best flours for a unique dough? What are the most common myths or mistakes when using yeast? And what about the differences between an electric oven and a traditional one? How to deal with heat, rising the dough outside or inside the fridge, or with gluten free flours? These are just some of the questions I have collected over the years on the web, to answer which I've thought of turning to real experts.

For a start, flours. They are always evolving, from the variety of grains and the diversification of uses, specific flours for precise doughs, strong or weak flours, whole wheat ones, mixed and gluten free, different compositions to obtain very different results. In the following pages, for example, you will have a full overview of flours with a high fermentation potential, that is to say, the type of flours capable of providing a digestible dough close to the pizzerias standard, or a briefer overview of flours available abroad. Moreover we will talk about how to store them at home and the tricks to work them at their best.

A second topic that we will analyze together with specialists will be yeast, a living creature without which we would have to give up the soft and fluffy pleasure of pizza. What is yeast actually, how does it work and, above all, how does it interact with other ingredients? Fresh or dry yeast, starter or brewer's yeast? And, perhaps, an even more important question: what are the most common mistakes when using yeast? A 'lively and fermenting' subject that never ceases to surprise.

Finally, heat – the ovens, tools that are increasingly decisive and evolving when talking about homemade pizza: together we will explore the differences between wood-fired, gas and domestic oven, we will also talk about temperatures and, above all, the various functions, including static, ventilated and humid mode, but also about the optimal cleaning and maintenance of the ovens, all essential factors for creating a good and healthy product.

Simple questions for us professionals that sound like impassable rocks for those who are not used to making pizzas as a job... so here we are, with the specialists of the sector, some of whom have been fundamental in my working life, helping me to understand not only how to best use these three very important 'ingredients' but also to control the causes, effects, timing of the procedures and the ways of interpreting them based on the results I wanted to obtain with more and more mastery.

Therefore, these insights will be the basis for understanding the world of pizza, in all of its contemporary facets and evolutions.

Flours

✳ *Traditional flours*

Davide Civitiello in conversation
with Mauro Caputo, Technical manager of Mulino Caputo

I met Mauro Caputo one day in July. We sat down and had a coffee by the seafront of Naples, with a view of Vesuvius. I've known Mauro for years and since forever I have admired his professionality, his know-how and his jovial attitude. Soon afterwords, we started talking about flour. I asked him straight away how was the flour for pizza created and which elements distinguish it from any other type of flour.

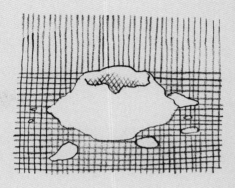

In the 50s, that is to say around the post-war period, thanks to the Marshall Plan the first packages of American flour began to arrive in Italy. Thus, the national milling compartment started to familiarize with flours characterized by a higher content of proteins, and selected Italian and European wheats so as to obtain a blend that would create the correct balance within the average strength, in this way obtaining a flour that would have precise rheology characteristics. With such a new product it was possible to obtain a great extendibility of the dough and, at the same time, also the strength and elasticity factors so functional for room temperature slow rising process. In fact, such characteristics are both crucial for the 'pizza' product because on the one hand one can easily work the dough to create a loaf – which must be touched the least possible before being baked – while on the other it is possible to obtain a better digestibility and a correct enhancement of the typical flavors and aromas of Neapolitan pizza, among other aspects. A social and cultural phenomenon such as the art of pizza making intersects with a highly specialized technological progression and a very rapid evolution. The 50s and 60s represent a radical change.

How did the Neapolitan pizza change with the introduction of these new flours?

The dough for Neapolitan pizza used to be mainly composed of weak flours. Therefore it was almost impossible to think about a rising process that could last longer than 24 hours. Indeed, the average time for rising was certainly more contained. Essentially, having a wider range of grains and cereals varieties at the service of the mills has been a factor that accelerated the growth of the segment, thus facilitating the gradual technological evolution, the experimentation and production of new flours and, as a consequence, of a different pizza in comparison with the past. Pizza has undergone and always will move towards a unique evolution. The types of ground flours used to be two only, that is to say zero flour and whole wheat flour. Then, by means of the sole use of mechanical processes, we have been able to separate in a more and more efficient way the bran from the heart – meaning the process of abburattamento (a refining phase) – thus obtaining flours with a lower content of ashes, the so called 'double zero flours'.

→ Basically, Mauro explains that, over the past century, this sector made bigger steps than those made over the last 20 centuries, a development that has always been based on empirical principles and, only at a later time, theoretical ones that led to the bases for the future bread-making processes.

Pizza has always been pizza. But pizza is almost like a work of art: it always has something to teach. The historical context has influenced the demand, and subsequently the offer. The diversification of the type of product – so prosperous today – depends on this aspect.

What do we mean by 'strength and structure' of the flour?

Strength is established in relation to the quantity and quality of the proteins contained in the flour, especially those that create gluten.

Gluten is a predominantly protein complex consisting of gliadins and glutenins that confer unique viscoelastic properties to wheat flour, distinguishing it from others, such as that of rice and chickpeas, which are unsuitable for prolonged manipulation and leavening.

The strength of a flour is then measured by specific mechanical tests directly performed on the dough – its extensibility and resistance – and it is indicated in technical jargon with a 'W'. High 'W' values identify so-called 'strong' flours.

When water and flour are combined, two elements get mixed: the ability of the dough to blend these two elements and to incorporate them by creating a compact structure defines the strength.

It is the same thing that happens in terms of the ability of the dough to hold the gas produced during the rising process. The strength of the dough therefore depends on both the amount of protein and the ratio of the protein components of that particular type of flour.

Strength is thus not a general theme, but it always depends on the

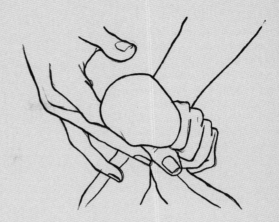

type of flour. A flour for shortcrust pastry, for instance, is not suitable for stressful conditions due to the fact that it has a weaker strength and a weaker level of gluten, producing scarce elasticity and stringing of the dough.

An extreme opposite is the flour used for panettone, as in this case the rising process is slower, more doughs come into play (between 2 and 3) and the dough undergoes various types of stress, thus requiring stronger flours with a higher level of proteins.

Imagine and compare the dough to a balloon holding air, and that can explode when the latter exceeds as the balloon is unable to contain it. Strength is the capability of that dough to hold air and to manage stress during the various production phases.

However, some proteins, among the different types of flours, have a greater ability to stretch, to incorporate water or create protein nets (e.g. gluten) that can retain gas and, so, the indicated 'W' is nothing but a pretextual measure acquired by the Chopin alveograph, a very common device utilized in mills. How does it work? The test consists in initially inflating the dough with some air. Then, before it explodes, the subtended volume of the dough is transduced in the form of energy (Joule) and, finally, in the form of this value.

How to choose the right flour for one's pizza. What piece of advice would you suggest?

In order to answer this question, it is important to first ask yourself several questions: what kind of pizza do I want to make? How long will my dough rise? Will I bake my pizza in a wooden oven or an electrical one? In essence, we must always buy flour on the basis of these three factors: the rising time, the type of cooking and the type of pizza we want to make. There is no better flour than the best flour for each type of dough. Indeed, there are very precise parameters so as to identify the correct type of flour and they are always indicated on the package of the product. Each flour has the exact answer for the right process, and the indications given on the package of the Caputo products, for example, are already calibrated on the basis of the consumers' specific needs.

→ The piece of advice that Mauro feels like suggesting me and all of you readers is to divide the selection of the flours into three phases: the first one consists in identifying the parameters and, thus, to know our mind on the type of pizza we want to make; the second step consists in reading and estimating with care all of the instructions provided by the flours producers on the packages, paying attention to the protein content indicated in the table of the nutritional facts; the third is to experiment continuously and to find the right balance so as to comply with one's needs in terms of taste. By means of this method, each of us will be able to find the most suitable flour for our future pizzas.

Which are the most common mistakes that end users commit when speaking about flour?

Considering the fact that we are not equipped with professional machinery at home, very often people run up against easily avoidable mistakes, just like using a very weak flour, such as an 'all purpose flour' – a flour suitable for each and every need – that is to say the most popular flour chosen over the last few years. As a consequence, the dough can easily stretch and spread, becoming gummy. In other cases, people tend to choose a far too strong flour that doesn't allow the dough to rise, limiting the expansion of the soft inside, creating a pizza with a very 'bread-like' cornicione (border) and very low in fragrance.

Precisely for this reason, during lockdown, we proposed a new type of flour that has been a great success, the Nuvola (Cloud), a flour with a very high fermentative potential, able to offer a very digestible dough and standards that are very close to pizzeria ones. This type of flour, with equal hydration, whilst cooking helps obtain the emptying of the cornicione, providing an inviting coloring tending to amber, which means a top-quality baking process due to Maillard's reaction.

Is it true that dough containing a lot of yeast does so that our stomach bloats?

The pizza yeast generally operates in optimal conditions between 22 and 26°C, and begins to suffer at temperatures above 40°C.

In general, when we cook a baking product the aim is to gradually reach an inner temperature of the dough of 80°C, catalyzing the gelatinization that, after the cooking phase, transforms the dough into what we usually call the soft inside of bread.

We then realize that when we bake our dough, yeast can survive the high temperatures of an oven only for a very limited amount of time, that is to say the time necessary for the cornicione to rise, thus creating an air pockets structure into the to then lose its fermentation activity. So the yeast concludes its mission and then deactivates, dispelling the myth that it can still act into our digestive system.

The question arises spontaneously: why is it advisable to use very little yeast for a more digestible and higher quality product?

The answer is not that easy to guess and it is necessary to consider some basic concepts regarding the chemical structure of flour in order to understand it.

Flour is mostly composed of wheat starch, that is a carbohydrate made up of amylose and amylopectin (respectively linear and branched molecules made up of glucose). Sugars play a fundamental role into the rising process because they nurture yeasts that, thanks to their hefty binges, produce both carbon dioxide – a gas that allows the rising in volume of the dough – as well as a little percentage of alcohol, useful in order to provide the right acidification of the dough, thus exalting flavors and aromas.

Till here, everything is quite clear. The problem is that the sugars belonging to the starch of the flour not always appear in a congenial form that allows them to get easily ingested by yeasts, and in this precise moment a further category of crucial actors for the rising process comes into play, that is to say those proteins present in all kind of food that by nature catalyze and accelerate various food processes: enzymes.

The enzymes of the flour are mainly 'amylases', and just like all enzymes in nature, they have a very specific task, that of breaking the bonds between the glucose molecules that make up amylose and amylopectin, releasing the simple sugars (glucose) necessary for the proper nourishment of yeasts.

I would like to highlight the fact that we are talking about enzymes that are naturally part of the wheat and the flour. We are likewise able to find them in milk, vegetables, fruit and so on and so forth. The same enzymes present in food are usually present in our digestive system as well; the amylases – for instance – are mainly present in our saliva.

In fact, carbohydrates in general must be chewed well as digestion begins in our mouth!

So, to take stock of this matter, if I do add a little yeast to the dough I will obtain a very slow and gradual gas release that, at the same pace, will provide the right time for the enzymes of flour to operate, making so that yeasts are always guaranteed a form of nourishment available, but also that the starch chains of the dough are broken so as to create a simpler and more digestible structure, a lighter structure that will facilitate the enzymes contained in our body, thus guaranteeing a faster and healthy digestion. Therefore, we can admit – using an aphorism – that a slow rising process with a low addition of yeast is similar to a 'self-digestion process' of the dough.

Many people from abroad are not able to find the suitable flours. What can you tell us about flours outside of Italy?

In the world of flours, these are officially and internationally classified by ashes and proteins. Ashes express the standards of mineral salts mainly contained into the bran parts of the cereals remaining in the flour after the 'abburattamento' process (meaning the mechanical separation of bran from the flour), starting from the double zero flours, characterized by a very low content of ash which as per the law must be under a percentage of 0.55%, ending with whole flours characterized by a high percentage of ash (and bran).

The alter ego of the '00' double zero flour in France is called farine de blè 550, in Spain Harina de Trigo T-55 and so on and so forth: the name may change but the substance remains the same, even though – with a patriotic sense – I am happy to declare that the double zero '00' leads the category very proudly for both completeness of the standards as well as levels of performance.

Proteins instead define the level of gluten of a flour, and proportionally its strength and tenacity. These two standards together can already offer approximate indications of the flour we are using. Obviously, to be as precise as possible, we would need more accurate data and analysis which define all the parameters in the ID of a flour.

We, at Mulino Caputo, have always believed in the diversification and specificity of flours. As I have already explained, the perfect flour doesn't exist, but there is always a perfect flour for each recipe. From this concept the idea to use symbolic figures on each package arises, a kind of image that would frame in a clear way the dedicated use of the flour.

In absence of such images, my advice is always to balance the level of strength and the rising time we adopt: the slower the rising process, the stronger the flour. Also in recipes requiring the addition of many fats to the flour, as it usually happens for desserts, I would suggest the use of strong flours.

Can you give any tips regarding how to store flours in the best way?

At home, flour must be kept at room temperature. It is better to store the packages on top shelves and far from any source of humidity, or other ingredients belonging to the same 'family' (durum wheat pasta, legumes, etc.) because flours can deteriorate due to infesting agents nearby. The insect of the durum wheat pasta or of legumes, for example, looks for a similar compound when ovulating, and very often flour is precisely the kind of context it looks for.

Another enemy when talking about the conservation of flour is humidity. A moister flour is more difficult to use in the dough. Moreover, humidity can facilitate certain inner biological processes that may alter the efficiency, thus almost entirely compromising the use of flour.

However, I would like to reassure you: a flour producer always tests the visible quality of the flour, that is to say the one that show in the hands of the artisan and so the reaction to the working process, but also the invisible quality, by means of microbiological, chemical and physical analysis.

The refrigerator can be used but it should never be set below 16-18°C. Flour is a living element and, as a consequence, it contains water.

The refrigerator can stiffen the flour and deteriorate the balance between strength and elasticity.

Flour must then always be kept into its packages, never above 24°C and never below 16°C, far from any other flour or similar ingredients, from humidity and away from the refrigerator.
In such optimal conditions flour can even last one year from the date of production.

Once the package of flour is open, can I mix it with another, different type of flour?

Flour is already a mixed compound! Many factories create – since the very beginning – wheat blends: various types and varieties from all over the world merge into one single blend and only later the producers try to adjust it, balancing all of the characteristics. This happens because there is no wheat in the world that already owns all the useful properties that allow use to obtain an excellent pizza.

It is experience – after all – that creates our 'perfect' recipe for flour!

There is already an indication regarding the scope of use on the packages of Caputo flour, thus it should not be mixed. However, it is also true that very often the consumer looks for a customized formula, able to satisfy the psychological and functional aspect relatively to his/her needs. So, in order to create some 'hybrid' mixtures it is necessary to pay attention and be precise as far as proportions are concerned, as taste, flavor, digestibility and an overall success of the product may be altered.

It is indeed useful to learn and deepen the research regarding the process and the ingredients because flour is already a recipe in itself, with diverse phases of manufacturing and, most of all, composed of various ingredients.

When flours are mixed we shall never take for granted that they will combine well as we may risk creating a dough that will fall short of our expectations. It is advisable to then mix flours only when we wish to create something completely unusual in taste. My only recommendation is to experiment continuously, until you obtain the desired result. And this is exactly what we do at Mulino Caputo, with the only difference that we use the most updated technologies.

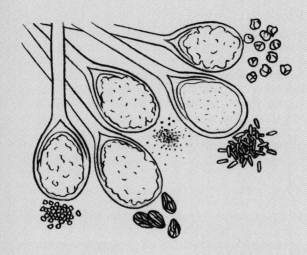

✳ *Gluten free flours*

Davide Civitiello in conversation
with Stefano Guerin, Mulino Caputo gluten free
research and development manager

Stefano Guerin is a leavening expert
and gluten free guru. We're meeting in a nice
restaurant in Bergamo Alta, at lunchtime.
Immediately, I go straight to the point and
ask him whether it is possible to make a good
pizza at home, even when it is gluten free.

Yes, it is possible to make a good gluten free pizza, even – and above all – at home. Just use raw materials or blends containing natural thickeners or fibers that make up for the lack of gluten. Still, should we compare a gluten free pizza to a traditional pizza, we must accept the characteristics of this specific type of product, and we should be aware of the fact that what will be tasted is certainly something different from the traditional product.

So what are the differences? What are the pros and cons of a gluten free pizza?

The main differences are essentially two: one of a technical nature and the other one of a gustatory kind. The preparation and processing of the product differ, above all, with regard to the time factor: a gluten free pizza does not need to develop a gluten mesh and, consequently, the processing times will be shorter. Gluten free flours are stickier. Therefore, the processing will be more complex and will occur with the help of special equipment. The advantage, however, consists in the fact that in a home kitchen you can safely use a stand mixer to prepare a gluten free dough considering that this kind of dough is not very tenacious. With no gluten, the dough needs less resting time and you can even make a tray-pizza in 2 hours only. Furthermore, gluten free pizza can be baked at lower temperatures although it requires a longer cooking time. Consequently, taking into account all these advantages, it is very easy to bake a gluten free pizza in a domestic oven.

What are the most common mistakes when making a gluten free pizza?

First of all, the main mistake is to compare the two doughs, trying to replicate the tenacity of the traditional one by adding less water or allowing it to rest for a very long time, or even kneading the product for 20 minutes. By excessively working a gluten free dough – which has a higher percentage of yeast than the traditional one – the yeast expands and consumes the sugars during the processing phase, dehydrating the product and making it so that it loses its color. Thus, the consumer is pushed to leave it in the oven for an excessively long time which will then toast the pizza and make it unappetizing. The traditional dough rises slowly and at room temperature whilst, as regarding the gluten free version, the rising phase begins immediately and an excessive rising makes it so that the dough bursts or even collapses. However, there is also a benefit, that is to say that gluten free doughs can be 'saved' more easily. When the product bursts, it means that the yeast has eaten most of the sugars and whilst cooking, the product will struggle to rise and we will not obtain that typical golden effect. Therefore, it would be ideal to let the gluten free dough rise for 6-8 hours, placing it immediately in the refrigerator, well covered so as to avoid dehydration. To make sure that the absorbing power of natural thickeners and fibers is not compromised, it is recommended to add fats (oil and butter) last. The preparation of a gluten free dough should take 5-6 minutes, organizing all the necessary ingredients in advance and with precision. Finally, the 'heat' topic: very high temperatures should be avoided, and we should always calculate a few more minutes when baking in comparison to the traditional pizza.

Is there a specific yeast for gluten free flours?

No, there is no specific yeast but I recommend dehydrated yeast because it is much more stable, both in summer and winter. A two-day fresh yeast, for example, will evolve differently than one that has been open for a week. On the other hand, dry yeast – when mixed with ingredients at their optimum temperature – can effectively guarantee constant results.

What piece of advice would you suggest as regards baking gluten free doughs?

As far as the ideal cooking for a gluten free product is concerned, there are no particular impediments on the type of ovens to be used, but one must pay attention to the rising phase, as we are dealing with a very sensitive and delicate product. The temperature of the dough should always be checked. When an overly warm dough enters the oven, during the first rising phase it can grow too quickly without structure itself and so, irreparably collapse.

Another key factor for baking is humidity which, especially in the initial phase, is very useful so that the dough rises. If my oven cooks too quickly and dries effectively, it could be counterproductive. Thus, the product may risk not growing and inexorably become toasted, which is why I recommend using the oven in a static mode for gluten free cooking (it is even possible to add a steel bowl with water to the base of the oven, especially when making bread, a product that requires a prolonged cooking).

What will the gluten free flours of the future be?

Alternative flours! Chickpeas, peas, corn, lentils, wholemeal (rice, buckwheat...) raw or steamed, and these can also be added to further types of dough providing such elements that, in the future, will be more and more precious, that is to say vegetable proteins and fibers. These flours bind at temperatures ranging from 60°C up and some of them, being a pre-cooked ingredient, are more digestible. In fact, these flours add and replace a part of the starches. Therefore, thanks to the technological advance in recent years, there has been a marked improvement in the production of gluten free products. About ten years ago, the use of deglutenized wheat starch was forbidden even in gluten free products. Whilst now, it is possible to use deglutenized wheat starch, guaranteeing values well below the gluten percentage of 20 ppm – part per million – or the threshold indicated by the Ministry. We can say that we are experiencing an important evolution in the gluten free world, especially in terms of taste and flavor, and this is something that also highlights the complexity and variety of the type of products that can be made from it. In a nutshell, the demand of gluten free products will increase because a highly diversified offer will also embrace and meet the needs of any consumer looking for naturally healthier products with a higher content of fibers, protein and vitamins.

Yeasts

Davide Civitiello in conversation
with Mauro Caputo, Technical manager of Mulino Caputo

One spring morning, so fresh and sunny, Mauro Caputo and I met around Piazza Garibaldi, near the central station of Naples. In front of us, delicious sfogliatelle for breakfast. We met to exchange a few words about yeast and its role in the pizza universe. There are always many uncertainties about considering the fact that yeast is a very complex ingredient, an element you need to know well to make a pizza that is worthy of its name.

How can we explain to the laymen what yeast is? And what are the types of yeast suitable for pizza?

Yeast is a single-celled eukaryotic organism (*Saccharomyces cerevisiae*) that belongs to the kingdom of fungi and literally comes to life from a by-product of agricultural origin, molasses. In fact, yeast can be obtained from a completely natural process, that is to say the aerobic fermentation of sugar, thanks to which this microorganism is able to live and reproduce. At the end of this process, when the microorganisms are sufficient in number and undergo the desired fermentation activity, yeast is marketed in a liquid form (yeast cream), as a fresh compressed dough or in the form of dry yeast granules.

The three types of yeast differ in the number of yeast cells contained in each gram, but they are all suitable for any baking product and pizza rising process. Giving an order of magnitude: a cube of 1 gram of fresh yeast contains over 10 billion yeast cells.

What are the main features and differences between fresh and dry brewer's yeast?

Fresh and dry brewer's yeast originates from the same cream of yeast which is subsequently dehydrated until it reaches 30-33% of dry matter, thus giving rise to fresh yeast, whilst as far as dry yeast is concerned the dehydration continues until it reaches 94-96% of dry matter.

In relation to the different dry matter of the two products, the content of live cells in dry yeast will be substantially higher than in fresh yeast, enhancing its rising activity.

In fact, dry yeast, thanks to its low concentration of water, can keep its fermentation activity stable for 2 years, at storage and distribution temperatures below 30°C.

Fresh yeast, whose water content is 67-70%, remains stable for a maximum of 45 days, at temperatures below 8°C taking into account the cold chain.

What is the difference between brewer's yeast and starter?

Brewer's yeast is a set of selected, highly performing cells that ensure a regular and constant quality in the rising of the dough, guaranteeing fixed dosages and processing times. With the use of brewer's yeast there is a faster and more constant rising process, with a more regular and easy to manage processing.

Starting from an already existing biological strain, starter is obtained by following the traditional method of refreshment: a piece of mother dough is taken and, by adding only water and flour in the course of operations carried out several times, a new dough is created with an optimal concentration of *Saccharomyces cerevisiae* and lactobacilli (bacteria that are not too different from those used in yogurt).

This consortium of yeasts and bacteria is then added to flour, water and any other ingredients so as to form the bread dough. While the rising action is largely carried out by *S. cerevisiae*, the bacteria lead to significant changes in the dough with beneficial effects for the shelf life of the product, its healthiness and its flavor too.

At what temperature should the different types of yeast be used so as to obtain an optimal result? Can yeast be frozen?

The optimal fermentation temperature of the dough ranges from 23 to 28°C. With temperatures close to 28°C fermentation times are shortened, whilst at temperatures of 23-25°C the times are lengthened, yet creating a moister and more fragrant bread.

As regards the freezing of yeast, it is strongly advised against, due to the fact that under a certain temperature the properties and effectiveness of the yeasts are altered.

Rising the dough outside or inside the refrigerator, what are the consequences?

The rising temperature affects the speed of the process and the 'maturation' times of the dough. In the refrigerator, rising times are lengthened and can range from a few hours up to 24-36 hours depending on the amount of yeast used, as well as the resting time of the dough, developing aromas and maximizing the action of enzymes. The time is longer but it allows more control over the process and the temperature. Very luckily this is the best solution for those who do not have a rising room at home.

What is the difference between the rising phase and maturation? And why does the dough collapse?

Rising is the result of the fermentation of *Saccharomyces cerevisiae* yeast that produces carbon dioxide — retained in the mesh (gluten) of the dough — thus the dough increases in volume. Maturation, on the other hand, is linked to enzymatic processes involving the components of the flour (starches, fats and proteins) and makes the dough more digestible, as the molecules are partly 'broken down' by enzymes and thus lighten the work of our digestive system. However, the two processes are correlated as maturation leads to the formation of simple sugars that are more easily used by the yeast itself: so, a correct maturation also contributes to optimal rising, in terms of colors and aromas. If the leavening/maturation times are excessively prolonged, the gluten mesh will weaken and the dough will no longer be able to retain gas, resulting in an excessive acidification and collapse of the dough.

What is *criscito* and when can it be used?

Criscito is nothing more than natural powdered yeast and has several functions. First of all, it acts as an improver of the dough during

the rising phase, it possesses an acidifying action, it creates favorable growth conditions for the yeasts, and it is fundamental for the stability and safety of the product because it protects it against molds, just like homemade sourdough – which basically contains the same microorganisms – but kept moist. Secondly, the *criscito* allows for the use of weak flours and acts on the gluten of the flour by means of lactic acid, permitting a more stable rising phase. As a consequence, the taste and aroma are improved, obtaining that typical flavor of natural yeast, because it brings organic metabolites such as acetic, lactic, succinic acid, which are formed during fermentation and carried out by yeasts and bacteria. Finally, the enzymatic action supports the hydrolysis of starch by breaking its long chains and forming simpler compounds (dextrins) that are more digestible and assimilable.

A question that many have asked me: can you freeze the dought balls?

Yes, the dought balls can be frozen. But frozen dough requires a different working method than a traditional pizza dough: it will be necessary to use slightly stronger flours and to increase the amount of yeast. The use of a blast chiller is ideal, in any case, the freezing of the dough must take place after the proofing phase of the balls that, once chilled, can be stored in a freezer and used preferably within a week.

The defrosting of the balls must take place gradually, so as not to run the risk of obtaining a far too moist dough.

Therefore, it is preferable to use a wooden pizza box and consider a resting time of 24 hours in the refrigerator before use.

Can you tell me what are the most common problems and mistakes related to rising? How can they be avoided?

The most common mistakes when creating a pizza certainly depend on the wrong choice of the raw materials. It is essential to be aware of the characteristics of the flour to better respect its maturation and rising times. Obviously, the other ingredients are also crucial in order to create an excellent product and, therefore, the correct use of brewer's yeast helps avoid many of the production risks.

The processing techniques are also fundamental for rising, but I personally believe that it is important to emphasize the role of temperature. In fact, a very common mistake, especially at home, is the approximate management of temperatures: pizza is a risen dough that requires specific timing and thermal conditions.

Therefore, the use of thermometers, scales and chronometers becomes as fundamental as the correct choice of ingredients and knowledge of the processing techniques.

All this leads to the creation of a product of the highest quality but also of great consistency.

Ovens

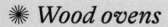 *Wood ovens*

Davide Civitiello in conversation
with Marco Acunto, CEO of Gianni Acunto Forni

I met Marco Acunto in August, in a fantastic
resort – seaside – on the Amalfi Coast.
We ordered an aperitif and started chatting.
Point blank, I asked him: why was pizza
born in a wood oven? Marco looked at me,
then he smiled and took off at a fast speed...

It's a bit like saying 'why were cars born with a diesel engine?'.
That was simply because an electric motor didn't exist yet!

But with one slight difference – the electric oven today has not yet
reached such standards as to cook a Neapolitan pizza; in fact, cooking
with wood brings a series of advantages among which prevails the heat
propagation. As a matter of fact, wood remains in contact with
the internal base of the oven (the ground) all the time, transmitting heat
not only by radiation but also by conduction and contact, which is still
impossible to achieve with electricity and gas. On the contrary,
with these two cooking methods, the 'platea' – meaning the base
of the oven – remains colder, thus is not able to cook the pizza
in the right manner and evenly.

Instead, the wood-burning oven, by heating the base evenly,
also allow the underlying part of the pizza to cook well.

Many think that smoke represents an advantage, others consider it a disadvantage for a successful pizza. What do you think about it?

As for smells and flavors, we can dispel that false myth that cooking
with wood is not the best method because of the fumes generated
whilst cooking. The common thought is that any contact with the fumes
may represent, and rightly so, a disadvantage for the flavor of the pizza
itself, whilst – actually – the contact with smoke never occurs at all

in wood-fired ovens. An optimal position of the oven, placed in unventilated places and corners, and the presence of a flue make it so that smoke can rise without making any contact with the pizza, that will take on two different colors – a lighter one (at the base) and a darker one (on the surface).

Wood-fired ovens are supported by the workforce of pizzaioli and enthusiasts who know how to manage such a specific cooking, safeguarding the technical and cultural heritage of the craft, and – as a result – the quality of Neapolitan pizza.

Why does the wood oven remain the standard for traditional Neapolitan pizza?

The cooking of the wood oven is preferred for Neapolitan pizza because it reaches much higher temperatures than any other type of ovens. The Neapolitan pizza cooks at 450°C and, therefore, the wood represents a quality standard. A gas-cooked pizza, on the other hand – as I have already said – involves some critical issues regarding the conduction of heat as the flame descends to the ground and heats up the dough, following a circular motion that disperses all of the heat on the floor. So, a pizza cooked with gas turns out to be undercooked on the base, even leaving halos of flour for a product not properly cooked. We tried to solve this problem by producing ceramic glass mats that retain heat and spread it homogeneously. However, it is necessary to mention that gas is increasingly becoming an important part of the work of those who manufacture ovens, whilst still occupying a smaller percentage of the production niches today.

The Neapolitan pizza, like everything in the kitchen, is evolving, shouldn't the same happen as far as ovens are concerned?

The evolution of awareness on issues such as environmental protection, air pollution and deforestation, means that companies like ours employ many resources in research and development so as to improve, increasing the production of less polluting equipment and, therefore, more eco-sustainable solutions.

It must also be said that the use of the wood-fired oven can cause some logistical problems, such as – for example – the mandatory installation of the flue, so difficult to install in certain structures, or the management of the wood itself, the difficulty in keeping it running smoothly. And precisely for this reason, thanks to the evolution of the dough, the electric oven has recently found its fortune!

In fact, the electric tends to dry much more than a wood oven – dehydrating a traditional dough more easily –, but with the new contemporary doughs, which are more hydrated and cook even at lower temperatures, in longer amount of time, the presence of an electric oven, especially a domestic one, can facilitate the production of excellent homemade pizzas – and much much more! – which are cooked evenly.

However, a true Neapolitan pizza requires a cooking standard that preserves the moisture of the ingredients and as a consequence, the typical and unmistakable flavors and aromas of this product too. Moreover, so as to obtain a good result in the final dish, the open flame system, as already mentioned above, requires that those who bake the pizza are competent in the matter, thus creating that indissoluble – and typically Italian – connection between labor, craftsmanship and the product that in the 'world of pizza' is not interrupted even during the cooking phase. Making pizza is an art, and I would like to add that professional pizza makers and bakers should defend their skills and tools, quite in the same way painters have always defended their brush and palette.

According to your experience, what are the most common mistakes made by pizza chefs and amateurs when it comes to ovens?

There are several mistakes that can be made when using a wood oven, especially during the cooking and maintenance phases. The oven is usually damaged due to the 'ground-cooking' of products that can be too moist: in this case, the oven absorbs water and the base tends to crack. Also, it is advisable to use wooden tools and stands rather than tripods or any other iron equipment. For traditional ovens, in fact, materials such as clay, terracotta and pozzolana have been used, requiring particular care. Even the wrong use of the peel, for example, can damage the base of the oven, or you can even make a mistake during the cleaning phase: the inside should never be cleaned with a wet cloth, but always with a dry one!

As for the cooking process, the errors can be many and various: leaving the oven on for a long time, for example, can cause the preparations to stick to the base, and not to maintain the right humidity, toasting the pizza or even carbonizing it.

The oven is important and needs continuous care, attention and certainly a thermometer to keep the temperature under control. Also, you must always keep a good management of wood, in abundance, because the oven consumes a great amount of it: first it darkens, then it becomes incandescent and only later, it reaches the right cooking temperature. I think the concept is now clear: 'automating' the art of the baker – and the pizza maker – means running the risk of losing the beauty, the complexity and truthfulness of the manufacturing process of an original Neapolitan pizza. The wood-burning oven is eternal, it can last for centuries, so the ability to preserve and 'take care of' it is essential!

Therefore, a wood-fired oven requires special precautions: it must be protected, it must be used often – as it also captures external humidity, so useful for cooking food gently- it must be covered well because it is often located outside people's homes, it needs time to reach the right cooking temperature, so it should be turned on long before (for example, in the early morning so as to be ready to cook at lunchtime).

Contemporary pizzas, homemade pizzas, ecological issues: what will be the trend of the future for the wood oven?

If you ask me, the trend of the future is already in place today: opting for a combined oven, using wood and gas, with a burner that can be assembled and installed in a few moments. By doing so, you can have the functionality and practicality of the gas oven and the charm and quality of wood cooking, depending on your needs and availability of time.

→ The aperitif arrives at the table and Marco, for the first time since we sat down, finally takes a break. The rapture that arises whilst talking about ovens makes me understand even more how great is the history and passion that lies behind every single Neapolitan pizza.

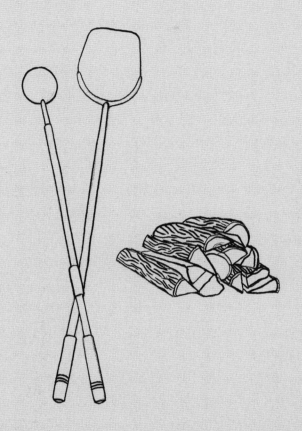

✳ *Domestic ovens*

Davide Civitiello in conversation
with Marco Zatti, Sell Out & Training Manager
Italy Cluster Electrolux Appliances

I'm meeting Marco Zatti via call. He answers
me from the parent company – Electrolux –
in Assago (Milan), and we immediately start
chatting about the importance of technological
progress relating to domestic ovens.

Marco, can you give me an overview of the consumption of domestic ovens in relation to pizza?

According to sales data from recent years, 20% of the consumers are directed to the purchase of ovens belonging to the medium-high range of the market, an equipment that combines traditional cooking and steam cooking at 100% humidity.

These data are symptomatic and help us to understand how much the tendency to have high-performance equipment has grown, even at home. However, we must never forget that there is also a medium-low range of ovens that still reach 250°C but do not retain liquids as much as the combined heat + steam ovens.

Humidity, in fact, acts as a vector that speeds up the penetration of the heat into the food, behaving as if the temperature in the oven was 30-40°C higher: which is of great importance when aiming to cook pizzas optimally.

Can you better explain the difference between these modes, static and ventilated?

The static oven was the first oven launched on the market and works with two resistances, an upper and a lower one, a factor that allows a 'steady and constant' heating through two hot zones: the game consists precisely in positioning food inside the oven depending on the desired cooking – more cooked on the surface or on the base. From the point of view of energy efficiency, however, the static oven is the most expensive because it requires more power for any cooking process; so the market has made a request of a different type of technology, a cheaper one, and companies have begun to produce convection ovens equipped with a fan that mixes the air coming from the two resistances, precisely the lower and upper ones. It should be noted that the upper resistor is almost twice as powerful as the lower resistor (1000 watts for the lower and 1800 watts for the upper). Then, the thermo-ventilated multi-function ovens were designed, introducing a third resistance placed around the fan. Instead of mixing the air, the latters is sucked in by the fan and then rejected on the third incandescent resistance, then exits the crown around the fan, in order to have more heated air flows. From the point of view of 'dry' cooking – meaning without humidity – this system is the most efficient, since there is no waste and a maximization of the heat output of the oven cooking is obtained, providing uniformity, cooking speed and saving in terms of energy consumption. So, as far as pizza is concerned, the best home cooking process would be that generated by the type of static oven because it is more controllable, even if less effective from the point of view of thermal efficiency and more complex as far as its use is concerned. In the static oven, manual skills, experience and control become indispensable variables and factors, and the thermo-ventilated oven mixes these variables a little, making the cooking process more difficult. Although technology is progressively improving from this point of view, dexterity, even in the cooking phase, is always the most important variable when it comes to yeasts, flours and derivatives.

How important is the use of the right tray when cooking a pizza in a domestic oven?

It is essential. Each material and element inserted inside an oven alters its cooking and efficiency. The ideal tray, for a pizza cooked in a domestic oven, would be a perforated and fairly thin tray. We, for example, produce a tray for desserts made of aluminum, with a non-stick upper part with many circular holes in order to support the pizza dough, which at the same time allows the heat of the lower resistance to cook the pizza in the best possible way, also on the bottom.

A Neapolitan pizza, on the other hand, is optimally cooked through the use of a refractory stone which, however, being very porous, is difficult to clean should an ingredient for a domestic preparation – such as mozzarella – leaks down, with the risk of getting dirty and not being able to be cleaned, as it cannot be cleaned chemically.

What is the best way to clean a domestic oven and perform an optimal maintenance?

Cleanliness is the decisive factor for the consumer! 15% of the ovens installed in Italy have a pyrolytic self-cleaning system, which works with a 500°C heating that carbonizes fats. Pyrolysis is the most effective cleaning system that reduces by 90% the effort of removing the dirt accumulated in the oven: thanks to carbonization, in fact, the user simply needs to clean the inside residues with a sponge.

Pyrolysis consumes about 6 kilowatts, constantly absorbing 3000 watts for the entire cleaning period (150 minutes). Finally, at the end of the pyrolytic cycle, it is important to clean the cavity accurately as residues of charred fat are toxic. The consumption of electricity used to clean an oven with this procedure costs about 2.00 euros in electricity and takes about 3 hours and a quarter of time. Data in hand, the average Italian user,equipped with a pyrolytic oven, uses this cleaning system only once every two years, regardless of the use of the oven, even if the appliance is used intensively.

But pyrolysis is not the only cleaning system, there are others. The most basic is the one characterized by hydrolytic cleaning: it consists in pouring 250 cc of water into the oven and allowing it to evaporate completely by turning on the lower heating element. The steam generated softens grease deposits, decreasing the difficulty of removing accumulated dirt with sponges and solvents by 30-35%.

High-end steam ovens (capable of producing 100% steam) are equipped with a cleaning system called 'intense steam'. The oven uses the steam generated by the boiler to effectively soften the accumulated fat and, thus, reduce in a decisive way the effort of removing it from the walls.

Compared to pyrolysis, the result is not very dissimilar, but certainly much more ecological since it uses much less electricity.

So what are the mistakes you shouldn't be making when cleaning an oven?

Well, using any unnatural method! Chemical and toxic solvents that can leave residues inside the oven must certainly be discarded. A dirty oven, besides the problems related to the alteration of flavors

and smells of the food being cooked, can be harmful, as the residual carbonized fats, as seen before, are toxic.

To avoid the accumulation of residues inside the oven, it would be useful to take advantage of steam cooking, in the various modes (high, low, steam only), which make an oven much less dirty.

Now, let's get straight into the 'baking' topic. Can you recommend any trick so as to bake pizza in an ideal way?

To bake a pizza in a perfect way, first of all, you must preheat the oven, bringing it to a temperature of 20°C above the cooking temperature; once reached, and the oven door is opened so as to insert the tray, the temperature will naturally decrease, reaching an ideal state for cooking.

As for Neapolitan pizza, it is advisable to use a refractory stone that allows you to keep the temperature constant throughout the cooking time.

Also, remember that a Neapolitan type of pizza cooked in a domestic oven must be placed in the oven garnished with tomato only; then, after two thirds of the way through baking, it will be possible to add mozzarella and further toppings. This will reduce the formation of water on the pizza without compromising a fine cooking of the base of the pizza.

Is humidity so important when cooking a pizza? Can you explain to us what happens exactly?

Our ovens have a 'pizza cooking' program designed for a thin pizza with a crispy bottom. This program uses heat in a static way by activating the lower and upper resistance and it demands that pizza can possibly be positioned on the first level, on a perforated tray: in this way the heat will pass in an easier way. The suggested temperature is about 220-230°C.

When cooking Neapolitan pizzas or classic thick pizzas, an oven needs the help of humidity. Humidity, in fact, helps cook the inside of the dough perfectly, as for the cornicione of the Neapolitan pizza or the inside of a thick pizza.

What to do if you don't have a steam oven?

If you only have a traditional oven available, without steam, we can resort to a trick: take a metal saucepan and, once filled with water, insert it in the oven in order to generate steam so as to perfectly bake a pizza. It is important to pay attention: to make sure that the saucepan generates the needed steam in the first cooking phase of a pizza, the water in the container must be very hot.

However, the pan cannot be used in all types of oven: there are such enamels not designed to be used with steam which can be damaged by the combination of high temperature and humidity.

So, how does a pizzaioli oven work?

The oven used by pizza makers does not need the addition of humidity because, thanks to the high temperatures (400°C) and the internal dome vault of the oven (which has a precise height) – also called 'water bottle height' –, it takes advantage of the humidity released by the topping of the pizza, creating a circular flow of humidity that helps to bake the dough optimally, especially where thicker. Through this process, the height of the oven, both for the professional wood-burning ovens and for professional electric oven, is – therefore – essential to obtain a perfect result.

There are legends and false rumors about ovens and their use... Can you tell me the most common ones?

As for the myths related to the oven, the most common is that of the maximum temperature. To bake a pizza in the best possible way, in fact, it is not necessary to use ovens able to reach 300°C as, on the contrary, they would compromise the baking process. There is no risk involved, instead, with small ovens available on the market and specifically designed for cooking pizza: they can reach a temperature of 400°C, and they are equipped with an open entrance that favors the frequent handling of the pizza, as it happens in the wood ovens of pizzerias.

Another false myth concerns cooking with the grill mode. In fact, it is commonly thought that this setting can be useful when the sauce is added on top of the pizza too late or, perhaps, in order to obtain an inviting crust on the vegetables that make any thick focaccia so rich in flavor: on the contrary, the grill does nothing but burning the product!

What is the future of the domestic oven?

The trend of the oven market sees a constant growth of steam ovens, a household appliance that, as we have seen so far, allows you to bake a Neapolitan pizza or thick pizza in the best possible way.

In the more advanced models of steam oven we also have the presence of a 'rising room' program which, at 35°C, at a controlled temperature, allows to accelerate the rising of the dough.

This program is, for sure, useful for a domestic process and I already know that many professional pizza chefs will turn their noses up when hearing 'rising acceleration', in their opinion, far too stressful for the dough. Professionals allow the doubt to rise between 24 or even 48 hours so as to obtain a perfect result.

→ Marco couldn't be more exhaustive and precise than this.

The new horizons of Neapolitan pizza

by Gennaro Esposito
Chef patron of the Torre del Saracino restaurant in Vico Equense (NA)

I met Davide for the first time in 2010-2011, in Tokyo. I was there for work and an entrepreneur friend surprised me by taking me to an event on Neapolitan pizza. Davide was about 26 years old and, on that occasion, he was there, along with the greatest pizza chefs of Naples, to promote one of the most famous Italian and Neapolitan dishes in the world. It was the first time I noticed his enthusiasm and desire to talk about pizza, as well as his attitude, so natural and competent. In fact, Davide is a person who doesn't talk much, but when he talks about his work, one immediately senses his passion, his unbridled desire to give and absorb knowledge. And with sentiment, devotion and a smile – in the end – he really managed to put pizza at the center of the world.

I am a Neapolitan cook, a chef who has been observing the subject for a long time from a privileged point of view, and what I can say is that, in recent years, there has been a true revolution in the vision of pizza: from an easy-to-access pop product it has gradually transformed in a dish of extraordinary complexity, though always maintaining that direct and immediate relationship with the people.

From a gastronomic excellence that could only be found in specific and characteristic places, the pizzerias, in the last period, pizza seems to have spread its wings in two other places of taste, haute cuisine and the domestic environment. It's a revolution, if we think about the fact that, until very recently, Neapolitan pizza could only be cooked in professional ovens and consumed in pizzerias, or as a tasty street food.

First of all, it is interesting to observe this new liaison between haute cuisine and pizza makers, it is a sort of evolution of the concept itself. For years, for example, pizza chefs have also become part of Festa a Vico, the event that we celebrate every year on the Amalfi Coast with young and established Italian chefs, and this is a clear sign of affinity between the two professions.

Now making a great pizza is like creating a great dish of haute cuisine, and perhaps it is even more so. Many factors come to mind, such as the management of the rising time, the temperatures, the different ingredients that interact one with the other... and in this game of time, cooking process and gestures, pizza actually reveals its almost illuminating side: afterall, pizza is a simple open disc that has the ability to simplify the analysis of the viewer – nothing is hidden in the pizza. In fact, everything is under the watchful gaze of the diner, unlike cuisine whose preparations often have hidden sides.

The evolution of pizza, on the other hand, is more physiological.

Although the following may sound like a strong expression, there is a very specific and regulated discipline regarding the subject and, in reality, there is not just a single traditional pizza. No recipe can exclude another in the everyday life of popular culture. There is no one way only of interpreting classic pizza: by only changing products, doses, cooking techniques, times and temperatures, the final result will be different.

And it is perhaps, precisely for this reason, that pizza has broadened its horizons, actually entering a new context of taste: homes, thus, a more exquisite amateur and domestic environment. This is perhaps the real contemporary innovation!

And so, the profound meaning of Davide's book emerges, which is not only didactic or based on 'notions', it is in fact a practical guide that offers different interpretations, several ideas that stimulate readers from all over the world to create new, original and personal doughs with their own hands. A game that never ends, a book that teaches and gives tricks, as well as professional knowledge in the presence of taste and of the gastronomic needs of anyone who loves pizza.

Once, it was unthinkable to reproduce a Neapolitan pizza (and in a tray) at home, because no one had studied how to do it. Davide did it, and he did it very well, too!

My wife, for example, was one of the first 'followers' of this way of narrating professional pizza, and reproducing it at home; by following Davide's instructions in the ItaliaSquisita videos, she managed to create a really good pizza and was very surprised by the result she had obtained. Under the pandemic we made so many and thoroughly enjoyed them!

Therefore, our houses became again a place to express the most solid and complex gastronomic culture. And pizza is certainly a dish that entered the homes from professional catering and can now be defined as a classic, a new classic, as young people would say.

After all, pizza is our gastronomic pride in the world and, in recent years, our Italian passion has made it so that the quality and the workmanship of this heritage has improved more and more, in pizzerias, restaurants and in street food abroad. I have indeed eaten more good pizzas than any typical Italian dishes outside Italy, more 'real' pizzas than crippled carbonara or amatricianas, and this says a lot.

Now, with Davide's book, this spring of pizza, tasty, nice and finally without errors, can also happen in all homes in the world.

Acknowledgements

In this book I talked about ingredients and procedures for making
an excellent Neapolitan pizza at home.
Precisely for this reason I want to dedicate it to the main ingredients
of my life, without which I would not be the man I am today.

To my mother Anna and my father Paolo, who have always believed
in me, supporting and encouraging me in every moment of my life.
Thanks to them, I safely guard all the smiles from my childhood,
I still keep the aromas and flavors from home.

To my wife Daniela, the woman who has always been by my side
and supports me every day. Thanks to her, I discovered the purest
and most sincere love. Daniela is an accomplice, a friend, a life partner
and, above all, she is a great mother, the best I could have ever wished
for my daughter.

To my daughter Camilla, the little woman who managed to reverse
the order of my priorities. It is for her and with her that everything now
has a deeper meaning. It is for her that I strive every day to improve
as a man, as a professional and as a father.

Special thanks to

Carmela Abbate
Carola Cappa
Antimo Caputo
Gianluigi Cardinali
Roberto Colombo
Assunta Coppola
Enzo De Angelis
Pietro De Marinis
Divise & Divise
Workline Divise
Franco Manna
Clelia Martino
Francesco Miccù
Pippo Montella
Miriam Pagano
Antonio Palmentieri
Giovanni Palmentieri
Massimo Passarelli
Andrea Segliani
Sabatino Sirica
Andrea Strati
Alexander Vollaro

Author
Davide Civitiello

General Coordinator
Alessandro Massi

Editorial Coordinator
Tea Capecchi

Editing
Carlo Spinelli
Francesco Inglese

Translation
Sara Locatelli
Marialuisa Iannuzzi

Graphic design
studio òbelo
Claude Marzotto
Maia Sambonet
Alice Guarnieri
Michela Meliddo

Illustrations
Beatrice Borso

Photo
Michelangelo Convertino

Printing
Papergraf International srl
Borgoricco PD, Italy

ISBN 978-88-945765-4-2

Published by

Vertical
Vertical srl